Career & Life Planning Guide

Career & Life Planning Guide

by JOHN W. LOUGHARY, Ph.D.

THERESA M. RIPLEY, Ph.D.

Follett Publishing Company / Chicago

Joan Willis, *Editor*
Robert Myers, *Designer*
Allen Carr, *Cover Design*
John Spottiswood, *Production Manager*
Gary Facente, *Publisher*

International Standard Book Number: 0-695-80678-5

Library of Congress Catalog Card Number: 76-17417

23456789/80797877

Contents

chapter 1

Life Is Just a Bowl of Cherries?

If the title of this book is intriguing enough for you to pick it up, then it is fairly safe to assume that some part of your life is less satisfying than you would like it to be. It's no secret that many people derive less pleasure out of living than they would like, and it is relatively easy to convince them that no one else has it quite as bad as they.

Your dissatisfactions may concern relationships with other people, goals which you have failed to reach, or simply those concerns with which you must deal from day to day. Most relationships, goals, and daily activities hold great potential for satisfaction, but they also offer the possibility of dissatisfaction. The chief reason we develop friendships; choose a spouse and have children; enter an occupation; and engage in leisure activities is the hope that these relationships and activities will add to the richness of our experiences. But things can go wrong. A person whom we expected to be a source of pleasure can become, instead, a source of annoyance, pain, or sorrow; a job that was once interesting or challenging can become boring or even threatening; a once-interesting schedule of daily activities can become monotonous.

There are, in other words, many reasons for people wanting to make changes in their lives; and they would if only someone would give them a second chance. Now, who in the world could really give you a second chance? No one. No one, of course, but yourself. True, you can't "start over," but you can provide yourself with an opportunity for a second chance—for making changes in your life which will lead to greater satisfaction.

Change is the name of the game in more ways than one. We all experience generally common life changes as we grow from childhood to maturity to old age. On the one hand, many of these changes offer potential for growth and increased satisfaction, and on the other for deterioration and mounting unhappiness and discouragement. There are also changes which you may desire and can bring about regardless of your age. These potentially self-initiated changes can be every bit as important as those which sooner or later all of us must experience.

It is not change itself which is the issue. Change is inevitable in some form. The important consideration in living a satisfying life is what you do about influencing the nature and outcomes of change.

For our purposes, we can view adult life as having certain stages, each ranging over a decade, more or less. One could easily find exceptions to these stages but, nevertheless, they can help clarify the various kinds of changes with which *Career & Life Planning Guide* is concerned. Let us begin by taking a very brief look at the changes which generally characterize each decade of the adult portion of the human life span. For our purposes, these stages begin with the assuming of independence for one's self and end with death.

The Early Years (20 to 30)

Beginning around the age of twenty and ending more or less by age thirty, most of us experience the initial adulthood stage. We finish our formal education and enter into a marriage or decide not to. There is concern about acquiring material goods and a home. There seldom seems to be enough money to meet personal and family needs, and job success is unknown. Occupational interest may be unstable and lead us from one job to another. For many women the restrictions of motherhood become firmly fixed, not to be shed for two or more decades. Friends become fewer in number, and job and family concerns leave less time for spontaneous recreation. The future seems infinite—it seems certain that there is plenty of time for all we want to do. Parents become part of the past. We and they now share adulthood.

It seldom occurs to us during these years that the earlier restrictions associated with the parent-child relationship may in the future undergo a role reversal. At work we are the youngest and sometimes resent the assumption that seniority and age automatically bring superiority and opportunity. We are often frustrated by the "system," knowing we could handle more responsible jobs if only we had the opportunity. Some of us try to obtain the good life in spite of our limited means and experience constant indebtedness. A few are required to deal with repossessions and bankruptcy. During these years many discover that marriage has its trials and problems as well as joys. Most learn that children bring serious financial and emotional obligations, and that the luck-of-the-draw by which they acquire friends can lead to problems. Our concerns for the development of our children can be difficult to express, let alone implement. Others, who were certain at the beginning of the decade that the single or childless life-style was the answer, occasionally have doubts about their decision as friends become more involved in raising families and less available as companions.

The first decade of adulthood offers many new opportunities and experiences. Some emerge from it pleased and eagerly anticipating the future. Others already have had a heavy dose of disappointment and are less optimistic about what the future will bring. A few have become resigned to a dreary and humdrum existence. Those who have survived the cultural shocks of marriage, family, and credit cards have taken a longer perspective of life, anticipating that the coming years will bring problems but that eventually they can be overcome and some day there will be smoother going.

The Building Years (30 to 40)

The second decade of adulthood brings new changes. We are no longer the youngest on the job, and many of those who are younger are obviously eager to challenge our worked-hard-for positions. The last of the children are born and some others leave the relative calm of childhood and enter the often tumultuous stage of adolescence. Those extra pounds put on during each of the past few years somehow total up, and losing them is not so easy. For some, occupational achievement has been significant and payoffs of professional recognition and financial remuneration urge them on to higher goals. For others, mostly women, the competition with the spouse's occupational or leisure interests becomes a serious but ill-defined contest. The rules of the game are unclear and appear to change with passing years.

Some people, with the leaving of children during the latter part of this decade of life, find that there is no reason for continuing a marriage. Many acknowledge that the differences between the payoffs of their life-style and those of their friends are becoming greater. This often leads to discouragement, envy, or jealousy. Making new friends becomes a rare event—everyone seems so preoccupied with their own concerns. Children become more outspoken; they request and sometimes take their independence without the experience and good judgment we know they lack. They want separate lives and balk at participating in family vacations. We want to trust them but sometimes wonder if it is wise.

During this second decade of adulthood we sometimes are concerned whether we have "done the right things" regarding family and self. A growing number of us are thinking less about our hopes and goals, preferring to pursue the pleasures of the moment. Many of us have invested ourselves heavily in the achievement of our children, and the returns may appear to be disappointing.

The second decade of adulthood involves the most dynamic changes in the adult life span. It begins for most with seasoned and relatively unencumbered youth and ends with firmly established middle age. Within these ten years we probably deal for the first time with more issues, problems, and traumas than we have ever faced before, or will face in the future. Many of us come to accept conditions which will determine our life-styles for the remaining years. This second decade of adulthood–from thirty to forty—passes quickly, and its importance is understood by most of us only after we enter mature middle age—forty to fifty.

The Transitional Years (40 to 50)

Most people probably have a common awareness during their forty-first year or thereabouts—it occurs to them that they are past the mid-point in life. **They have lived more years than they have remaining to live.** Time, consequently, becomes more valuable. There probably won't be enough of it to accomplish all that they would like. That they have failed to make those changes which they have been meaning to make for the past ten years is a preoccupying thought. It is clear that influencing the lives of some of their children is no longer possible. They are well on the way through their own journey of adulthood and drift farther away each year. Others, who have yet to cast off from the security of family, may seem even more difficult to reach.

Some have nagging second thoughts about their choice to remain single or childless. It becomes clear to many that they have reached the end of the occupational ladder, and that it didn't extend as high as they had hoped. It is obvious to many that they have reached the peak of their earning power, and that dreams of foreign travel and material possessions will never be realized. There will probably never be a trip to Europe, a South Seas cruise, a vacation cottage, a business of their own, or early retirement. Health takes on greater importance. If the physical process of aging has caused them no problems, it is beginning to affect their peers. They seem to know an increasing number of people who are on medication; who become hospitalized; who must restrict their diet and physical activity; or who have some serious health problem.

But as they reach the end of their forties, **new opportunities and freedoms appear possible.** The family is grown; the basic material requirements are less; and there is usually more money left after the bills are paid than ten years ago. There is a certain basic relief to having survived the past two decades. For many, there is less pressure, both from outside and self-imposed. What doesn't get done today or this week seems less important than in the past. As the fiftieth year approaches for many, there is a more reasoned view of the past; some regrets remain but there is the realization that what is past is past, and that whatever is to be gained from life must be drawn from and built in the future. Those routines established during the last two decades can soon be altered. But altered how? What are the options. There has been such preoccupation with doing, with surviving that some have forgotten how to dream and how to identify new paths. As the bondage of family is lifted, many feel lost and directionless—freedom is difficult when it is suddenly thrust upon them. Some recover quickly from the initial shock and set their sights anew, and others flounder for a time. But there is also a growing urgency to enjoy life, to not waste the coming decade, the end of which may begin the decline of life. The fifties, then, must be used wisely and to their full potential.

The Mature Years (50 to 60)

Some set out to capture the potential of this decade by attempting to return to a former. Others have no regrets about the past, and eagerly begin to enrich their lives with new experiences. The activities which result, however, may be the same. Health diets, weight reduction and physical fitness schemes, establishing new relationships and abandoning old, new personal grooming efforts, and self-improvement programs ranging from serious reading to learning new athletic skills all represent attempts to extend and enhance satisfaction with living. Sometimes these efforts bring about their desired outcomes; sometimes they simply use up time; and sometimes they are unrewarding and abandoned.

The fifties can be a decade of increased isolation, loneliness, and depression. Some have all but given up and can't seem to muster the resources necessary for rejuvenation. Death, in addition to divorce, now becomes a more potent source of losing spouse and friends. Old patterns of behavior seem more difficult to abandon; there seems to be less energy. The younger generation becomes a reality. We finally are convinced that twenty-one-year-olds don't really look any younger than they did when we were twenty-one. In spite of the many pleasures involved, becoming a grandparent can be discomforting. After all, didn't we once think of grandparents as "old people" and we certainly are not old—no sir, not by any stretch of the imagination. "One is only as old as one thinks" (nevertheless—grandma and grandpa we are!).

While some maintain their positions of leadership at all levels of family and work, many more find the reins slipping to younger hands. Requests for advice may be fewer. Toward the end of this decade we may realize that we have moved out of the mainstream; if the current is less demanding so are the challenges. Many of our friends "age noticeably," others take pride (and some secretly marvel) in the fact that they have changed little over the years.

Resolutions to give up bad habits and establish good ones are made more frequently as the close of the decade approaches. It is now clear that autumn is nearer than spring. Upon this realization, some value and guard time even more zealously; others become more detached. A few become bitter about the treatment which life has given them. The irrational—those who blame other people, events, and circumstances for their status in life—tend to become more irrational. And those who have learned to accept responsibility for themselves and who strive to determine their own destinies tend to retain a realistic optimism about the Golden Years.

The Golden Years (60 Plus)

It is not only chronology which makes the difference during the sixty-plus years, but also one's perspective, state of mind, or mental health. Some of us are psychologically and mentally dried up at sixty (or before) and others are alert and dynamic at ninety (or after).

Nevertheless, the golden years hold for most of us retirement, Medicare, physical deterioration, maturity of grandchildren, exclusion from leadership and other participation, increased experience with death, relatively huge amounts of discretionary time, and dependence on those who once were dependent upon us. We have the time so much wanted in youth, but without many of the resources of youth.

No one has expressed it better than George Bernard Shaw: "Youth is a wonderful thing; what a crime to waste it on children."

While many use the golden years to extend and enhance life and the satisfaction they derive from it, others find it a time of loneliness, boredom, and a waiting room for death. Those past sixty often find themselves misunderstood by those who have yet to experience the conditions of retirement and all that is associated with the golden years—and that is only natural. Each of us has the experience of our own generation, and all but those in the golden years of life have at least one generation to look to which has been through their current experiences. Those in the golden years, of course, do not; there is no group of people who have had the "golden years' experience" and then moved on to another phase of life. This may account in part for the glowing picture often painted of the years past sixty. The term itself has come to suggest a period of quiet, soft existence in which cares and responsibilities are few, and time is abundant for contemplation and doing all those things which one always wanted to do. Many senior citizens would label such a suggestion "nonsense!" and would add that old age is just that—*old* age.

THE PURSUIT OF SATISFACTION

We have tried to illustrate that no matter what the stage of life, one not only encounters new problems and challenges, but also new opportunities for increasing the satisfaction derived from living. The message is not original. **Life involves continuous changes.** Some are part of the life cycle and cannot be avoided, and some which have little or nothing to do with external events can be initiated.

The key to leading an enriched life is the ability to effectively manage those changes which are an inescapable part of the life process, and initiating other changes which will maintain and increase satisfaction.

As this is not the first time this observation has been made, neither is this the first book addressed to the issue of life change and satisfaction. Many are available, each at least implicitly offering some guide to self-help. There are generally three approaches taken by self-help books.

The first approach essentially offers sympathy and condolence. By overwhelming readers with descriptions of the trials and tribulations of miserable people it is hoped that they will see that relative to these miserable souls, their own situations aren't nearly as bad as they had believed. Books taking this approach offer no specific suggestions, although many imply that readers can learn from observing the mistakes of others. Many people enjoy reading books taking this approach; it is probably true that misery does love company.

A second method used in self-help books might be called the case-study approach. These books often relate the stories of people who have overcome dissatisfying and even traumatic circumstances in life, ranging from successful but dissatisfied executives who escape to tropical islands to paraplegics who become successful and satisfied executives. The stories they tell are meant to be inspirational and carry the implication that the readers may apply such actions to their own lives. Many people enjoy these case studies and apparently find within them a source of motivation.

The third approach used by books concerned with helping people make changes which will lead to greater satisfaction with life might be termed the how-to-do-it perspective. Such books offer little sympathy and condolence and few if any heroes and heroines after which readers might model their own behavior. They tend to offer suggestions and ideas, and to describe skills for making life changes. *Career & Life Planning Guide* falls into this third category. Whether you can profit from reading *Career & Life Planning Guide* depends on the extent to which you are seeking sympathy, inspiration, or specific suggestions for making changes in your life.

Our intended audience is people who can accept the position that the source of change in your life is you, and that you are more likely to make desired changes when equipped with certain ideas, skills, and information, than when supported by sympathy and inspiration. Clearly, that position is neither attractive nor acceptable to many, and that is fine.

Because we do not want to mislead or disappoint readers regarding our intentions, we try to be clear about our purposes from the start. If you are willing to make lists, complete exercises, and practice skills we will describe, then there is a good chance you will enjoy *Career & Life Planning Guide* and find it useful. If, in other words, you are willing to become involved in the book and actively participate beyond reading its words, then it's you to whom we are writing. If you find this kind of participation uninteresting or tedious, then *Career & Life Planning Guide* is probably not for you. Whatever potential value the book may have will result from readers "interacting" with us by doing the suggested activities—not just reading about them.

Thus, if you are willing to invest some thought and effort to *work* at changing your career (life) then let's be on with it. **Life may not be one big bowl of cherries, but it can have its sweet times.** It's up to you.

chapter 2

Careers and the Great "Perfect Job" Myth

In the following pages we will be concerned with certain ideas, skills, and information regarding career change. Because the term career is used in the broadest sense (we're talking about life) we should have a mutual understanding of the word career and several related terms.

Historically, a career was defined more or less as how one earned a living. Thus, career was synonomous with "occupation"—or job. A career was being a banker, nurse, teacher, clerk, factory worker, secretary, or housewife, for example.

The historical definition of career as an occupation is in large part a reflection of economic and social conditions. The work day and week formerly consumed a major part of one's time. Most of the remaining hours were needed for self and family maintenance.

These circumstances are now changing for an increasing number of people. The work week is shorter; many jobs are less demanding; and an increasing number of people are over-educated for the jobs available to them. Self and family maintenance are not as time-consuming as previously.

In short, **for an increasing number of people, a career means more than an occupation or job.** We can define career as those major activities which are of prime importance during one's life. We can also identify three kinds of major life activities:

(1) Job—activities which contribute to basic survival needs (i.e., making a living)

(2) Vocation—activities which provide a sense of self-fulfillment, self-worth, or contribution

(3) Leisure—activities which contribute to recreation and aesthetic pleasure

For some people one activity can serve all three purposes. For example, the activity "teaching" provides an income; most likely provides a sense of self-fulfillment; and may even at times be fun to do. On the other hand, driving a gravel truck may serve only to provide an income. The truck driver may do leather craft as a means of achieving self-fulfillment, and turn to bowling as a chief leisure activity. Even though the specific nature of a career differs with each individual, a career is often more than an occupation. To repeat, **a career consists of those major activities which are of prime importance during one's life.**

The definitions just given for *job* and *leisure* are pretty obvious. But you may be somewhat puzzled over our definition of "vocation"—namely, "those activities which provide a sense of self-fulfillment." You may say, "Why not use the term avocation?" That's a reasonable question and there's a good answer. Our intent is to emphasize the idea that the most valued activities in one's life—his vocation, if you will—can having nothing to do with earning a living. Given the relative affluence which surrounds many of us on the one hand, and the boredom inherent in many jobs on the other, more people will turn to non-job (that is non-paid) activities to gain a sense of worth, contribution, meaning, or self-fulfillment. Such activities, furthermore, should not be viewed as "extra" or avocational. Given an adequate income level, such activities can be the most meaningful in life.

Once people accept minimal levels of career development, they become content to live with vague feelings of discontent. They become indifferent to opportunities for gaining more from life, and are the chief obstacle to their own personal development. In career planning we often encounter people who indicate that "I'm nobody," or "I couldn't do that," or "That's only for other people, I'm just average." They have, in other words, constructed a very effective barrier to career development.

One purpose of this book is to assist readers to clarify this concept which we refer to as a sense of vocation. Another is to suggest various ways of overcoming barriers to career development and begin implementing more satisfying vocational aspects of career development.

The practical importance of the distinction between job and vocation is to separate job hunting and vocational planning as two often related, but different tasks. When one's job must also be the chief source of self-fulfillment or when one's vocation must also provide an income, needless constraints are imposed.

The following examples may help clarify the usefulness of the job-vocation-leisure concept of career.

John has a college degree in creative writing. According to his former professors, he is a competent writer. Perhaps more important, he has sold several short stories to magazines. John is a realistic fellow and accepts the fact that professional fiction writing is extremely competitive. He has a family and desires a standard of living for the family which requires more than a bare subsistence income. If he didn't have this value, he might devote most of his time to writing and depend upon part-time jobs to provide minimal subsistence. That would be fine for some, but John values his family life. Consequently, he obtained a job as an administrative assistant. The job is not unpleasant, and it provides a satisfactory income. However, if you asked John to identify his vocation, he would tell you that he is a writer. He devotes an hour or two each evening and usually one day each weekend to writing. His fantasies about success focus on writing. His major feelings of accomplishment come from having a story published, or even from feeling that he has written a good piece. Observe also that he doesn't hate his administrative assistant job. At times it is challenging, and he enjoys the people with whom he associates. He also engages in purely leisure activities such as reading, watching television, and hiking.

Mary presents a different career mix of job-vocation-leisure activities. Married and twenty-six, she is employed as a secretary. She derives both an income and much enjoyment from that activity. If, however, you asked her to name the most important part of her life (her vocation) she would probably tell you, "wife." At this point in her life, Mary's main concern is working at her marriage; her main payoffs are successful events in her marriage relationship. What about leisure? In Mary's case her leisure activities are so interwoven with her marriage (vocational) activities as to make the two inseparable.

Joyce is a work addict. She is employed as a teacher, an activity by which she earns a living. The various tasks she performs as a teacher are also her chief source of accomplishment and self-fulfillment. Teaching is her vocation. And what about leisure? Strange as it may seem, Joyce most prefers to spend much of her free time developing instructional materials. It is a relaxing and pleasurable activity for her.

Finally, consider Bill who works as a computer operator. He has a job, but little else. The job is pleasant but offers no challenge. It is something he doesn't mind doing, but he derives no particular sense of accomplishment from it. His sense of commitment is nil. Accounts receivable makes little difference in his life. What does turn him on, if not operating computers? Unfortunately for Bill, not much. Then he must be a leisure freak? No, not even that. After work Bill stops for a drink at a neighborhood lounge, goes home, scans the paper, glances at a current magazine, and then stares uninvolved at the tube until going to bed. Bill has a job, and that's about it.

One can assume that John, Mary, Joyce, and Bill all engage in some common activities such as reading, interacting with others, and working. They are different, basically, in regard to their perception of these activities. As a result, in part, they have developed different kinds of careers, as Table 1 illustrates.

TABLE 1. Career Activities

	JOB	VOCATION	LEISURE
John	Administrative assistant	Writer	Reading and outdoor activities
Mary	Secretary	Wife	Wife
Joyce	Teacher	Teacher	Teacher
Bill	Computer operator	None	None

A further note regarding Bill's career may be helpful. Even if he doesn't have a vocation, doesn't he engage in leisure time activities (note the TV watching)? No, not in terms of this concept of career, because he does this activity without purpose. If he viewed TV for educational or entertainment purposes it would count as leisure or even, perhaps, vocation. But in terms of our concept of career, it is only a means of killing time. Because it doesn't produce any other reward, it simply doesn't count as a career activity.

Finally, let's be reasonable regarding the amount of self-fulfillment people desire. Some have a passion for contributing to the well-being of others and never seem able to do enough. They fulfill their potential through giving. Others, equally determined to realize their potential, do so through personal experiences such as reading, music, art, and travel—none of which contributes a drop of good to the well-being of others. At the other extreme are those people who never heard of self-fulfillment. Given sufficient food, drink, sex, and entertainment, they're perfectly happy and content.

Most of us probably fall somewhere in between these two extremes. We do want to feel that something in which we are engaged is personally rewarding, or that it makes a difference to someone else, or both. To the extent that we do, we have a sense of vocation. And, as we shall see from time to time in the following pages, one person's vocation is another's job, and both are leisure activities for a third person.

HOW MANY CAREERS IN A LIFETIME?

How many careers do we have in a lifetime? Only one, in terms of our three-dimensional definition of career. **Rather than thinking in terms of a different career, it seems more useful to think of making changes in your present career.** Changes can be major, as in the case of a retired military officer who becomes a teacher; or minor, as in that of the housewife who joins a book discussion group.

When does a career begin? From the perspective used here, it starts when we enter kindergarten or first grade. Certainly it is clear that the preschool years are extremely important as a foundation for personal development. Some claim that what happens during these years practically predetermines (in a general sense) the remainder of our life. Nevertheless, something of critical importance happens when we first enter school. Namely, we move from a single institution base (home) to a double institution base (home and school). We become more accountable for our own behavior; experience greatly increased opportunities to make independent decisions; and most important, confront the life-long process in which each self deals with and attempts to survive in the larger public. Some of this takes place prior to entering school, of course. Nevertheless, the magnitude of the dependence on and risking of self which occurs when we begin school is the reason we have identified that event as the starting point for careers.

The fact that children themselves recognize this concept of career was beautifully illustrated by a small group of fourth graders who were participating in a classroom lesson. The topic was careers. Toward the conclusion of the lesson the teacher asked the group, "Do you have a career now?" "Yes," replied a little girl, "I go to school and play the violin." "Sure," answered a boy beside her, "I go to school and play Little League."

From this point on, each of us experiences a variety of career changes. Some of these are made in response to events beyond our control, and others are internally motivated. The changes occur each time that major activities are altered. Examples of changes include moving from elementary to high school; from high school to college or work; from one kind of work to another; from being single to married; from non-parent to parent; from married to divorced; from interested in sports to uninterested in sports; from active in community affairs to inactive in community affairs; and from a parent living with children to one whose children are gone. All of these examples represent common career changes. In each change, however, only certain aspects and behaviors in one's life are altered. Much of what was before remains. We may change jobs but still function as a spouse and parent. We continue to deal with the responsibilities these activities entail. When the last child leaves home, certain changes in life activities occur but many others continue unchanged.

Thus, it is important to think in terms of a lifelong career in which a number of changes in activities, shifts in responsibility, and emerging and disappearing interests and values occur. Not everything of importance changes at any single point. A career is a complex continuum, and changes represent highs and lows not total beginnings and endings.

There is, in this lifelong process, some degree of irreversibility. It is true after all that you cannot go home again. Not completely. You change and so does home, so it's never quite the same. Signs of irreversibility appear early in careers. The child who didn't learn to read well in elementary school, but who suddenly "caught on" in high school has a more difficult time preparing for college than her peers who did read effectively by grade six or seven. The high school student who took a general course load and then decided during his senior year that he wanted to attend college and become an engineer will discover that acquiring the prerequisite math and science skills upon which admission to an engineering major depends is difficult. The middle-aged housewife with a high school education who decides she would like to go to work but has no sellable skills cannot turn back the clock. It is true that she will encounter more difficulty obtaining training and employment now than twenty years ago.

We cannot undo the past. But that is not to say that past behavior or lack of it always places irreversible limitations on the future. There are often ways to compensate for lack of experience, for past decisions which appear unwise, and for many kinds of disadvantages. The challenges in doing so can be stimulating and rewarding. The concept of irreversibility as applied to career change, nevertheless, is important to keep in mind as a means both of bringing realism to career change hopes and as a stimulus for imaginative alternatives.

VOLUNTARY AND FORCED CAREER CHANGES

Table 2 illustrates a variety of common events and situations which stimulate people to make changes in their careers. As it shows, some career changes are done on a voluntary basis and others are, in a sense, forced. Both kinds constitute adjustments in major life activities. Even though the circumstances accompanying forced and voluntary career changes may appear very different, the same general process occurs. Forced changes are often precipitated by dramatic and unanticipated events such as job loss or physical injury, and there is usually less time to plan than in voluntary change. Further, the individual

TABLE 2. Some Common Reasons for Career Change

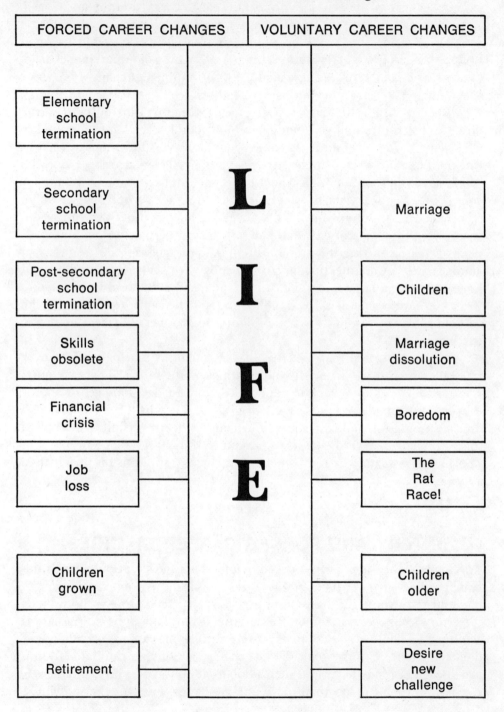

FORCED CAREER CHANGES	VOLUNTARY CAREER CHANGES
Elementary school termination	
Secondary school termination	Marriage
Post-secondary school termination	Children
Skills obsolete	Marriage dissolution
Financial crisis	Boredom
Job loss	The Rat Race!
Children grown	Children older
Retirement	Desire new challenge

L I F E

initially may be preoccupied with the precipitating event. On the other hand, the person in a forced change situation is often strongly motivated.

Voluntary career changes are not usually precipitated by a single traumatic event. Those contemplating a voluntary change most likely have given it some thought over a period of time. In some cases the voluntary change is anticipated, as illustrated by a mother who knows that in two years her last child will be in school. She may predict that with the lifting of constant child care responsibility she will have increased freedom and opportunities to pursue new activities and to begin planning for the future. Other voluntary changes are not so clearly anticipated. Instead, they grow out of an increasing dissatisfaction with one's situation. Career changes resulting from marital dissatisfaction and job boredom are examples of these kinds of voluntary changes.

It is not uncommon—or unnatural—for someone wanting or needing to make a career change to feel isolated or to suspect that they are alone in their career change concern. This simply isn't true; they are not alone. Consider, for example, the number of people in the U.S. who made the following kinds of career (major life activity) changes in 1972. Using information from the *1972 Statistical Abstract,* we can estimate that:

2,270,000	got married
840,000	were divorced
3,200,000	finished high school
981,000	completed college
632,000	joined the service
308,000	were sent to prison
303,000	were released from prison
36,541,000	changed place of residence
3,256,000	added a baby to their household

Career change, then, is a relatively common event.

As many readers will be quick to point out, career change can be precipitated by multiple causes—forced, voluntary, or a combination of both. Regardless of the cause, however, it is clear that the vast majority of people will experience significant changes in their careers. The question then is not whether to change but, rather, will the change be effective?

EFFECTIVE CAREER CHANGES

What constitutes an effective career change? Each instance is different, of course, but all can be measured by two general criteria. First, an effective career change should result in the achievement of your goals. Second, and equally important, an effective career change should not generate new sources of dissatisfaction.

There are several general concepts or guidelines for making effective career changes upon which the material in the following chapters is based. These guidelines emerge in several forms and in various contexts throughout the book. It should be helpful, nevertheless, to examine them briefly at this point.

Know What You Want

Jim Brown was employed as a shoe repairman. He is married and the father of two children. During the last two years he had become frustrated over the lack of variety and challenge in his life. His unhappiness began to show at home as he became increasingly irritable toward his wife and children. The obvious solution which occurred to Jim was to obtain a more interesting and challenging job. After exploring several possibilities, he accepted a job as a routeman for a bakery. He anticipated that the variety of public contacts, the challenge of a small sales commission opportunity, and the variety of tasks involved in the job would provide whatever was missing from his life.

It didn't. Jim discovered that he dislikes the competition with routemen from other bakeries. When the weather is stormy, he is wet and cold much of the time. While he has contacts with many customers, he has found that he misses the comradeship with fellow employees in the shoe repair shop. He also has discovered that he has less control over his time. The former job was limited to 9:00 A.M. to 5:30 P.M., five days a week. As a routeman he begins at 7:30 A.M. and frequently doesn't finish until 6:30 P.M., and often must work on Saturday.

Looking back to his original decision, Jim recalled that his initial goal was "to obtain a more interesting and challenging job." With the aid of hindsight, he realized that he had not stated his goal very clearly. A clearer statement would have been "I want to become involved in activities which will provide me with some personal challenges and a feeling of accomplishment."

Achieving that career goal, of course, might or might not involve a job change. For example, he might have joined a service club, an ecology group, or a conservation association as a means of becoming involved in activities which would be challenging and meaningful. But the manner in which he stated his initial goal confused it with one possible means of achieving the goal—a job change.

One means of assessing the extent to which we understand a career goal is to ask ourselves whether we have described an outcome (s) or a particular means of achieving the outcome. If it is the latter, try again. Keep your options open.

Count Your Resources

An otherwise potentially effective decision to make a change in your career may be scuttled by lack of resources. The most important kind of resources usually consists of skills, information, and finances.

Changing jobs often requires learning new skills. As obvious as that may seem, many people float from one unsatisfying job to another without first acquiring new skills. They have no more to offer the new employer than the last. Many times the problem is having skills which one can't use in a given job, and that's a different issue.

Information is a resource in the sense that it allows you to predict the requirements and conditions of an anticipated change. For example, the failure of many people to complete correspondence and night school courses is due to their lack of information regarding the amount of study time involved. One former client is typical. She enrolled in a secretarial course only to find that its successful completion required about three hours of study per day. Her other responsibilities simply prevented her from finding the time. If she had obtained this information prior to enrolling in the course, she could have arranged her time differently or taken a smaller course load.

Information can also have important implications for changes in the vocation and leisure aspects of a career. One of the authors, for example, seeking greater family participation in a common activity enjoyable to all, purchased a used, eighteen-foot boat. Anticipating fishing trips and family cruises on the bay, he quickly learned among other things that: (a) used boats need constant upkeep; (b) they frequently break down at just the time you want to use them; (c) boat repairs are expensive; and (d) one encounters a variety of risks when boating in tidewater. The outcome was disappointing, if not disastrous, and the boat was sold (at a loss). All of this information was easily obtainable prior to the career change decision.

The need for financial resources in regard to career change is often underestimated. Either due to lack of experience, wishful thinking, or unanticipated events, career change efforts can be rendered ineffective when funds run short. Many financial advisors suggest that after carefully estimating the costs involved in a life change, one should then double the amount. Whether this is always sound advice may be questioned, but estimates of financial resources required for a career change are often inadequate. The American dream of "finding a little place in the country" serves as an instructive example. The family that makes this kind of career change may discover significant and unanticipated increases in the cost of transporting children to school and town, insurance, household repairs and maintenance, and the need to purchase equipment necessary to cultivate their land. Such a change may meet our first criterion of an effective career change (making more satisfying activities available) but at the same time generate financial problems which cause significant new dissatisfaction.

Know the Risks

Risk refers to what one might lose or forfeit as a result of taking a particular action. With regard to contemplating career change, it is important to identify what one stands to lose. Risks include financial and material goods, personal relationships, self-esteem, security, freedom, and a variety of other intangible considerations.

Risks are involved in successful as well as unsuccessful career changes. That is, you can lose whatever you risk regardless of whether you reach your career goal. Consider, for example, two men who changed to more demanding but higher paying jobs. Because of the demands of their new positions, each man had less time to devote to his family. In that sense both risked family relationships when they made changes which would increase their incomes. One man was successful in his new position but was divorced by his wife within two years. The second man failed in his new position, and as a result, his wife also left him.

Be Honest with Yourself Regarding Values and Feelings

Career changes made by people who are not being honest with themselves are often futile. Values and feelings are integral parts of most career changes. When they are ignored, the change may be superficial at best—at worst, pointless and a waste of effort.

People often avoid dealing with their values and feelings because it can be a painful process, because resolution of conflict seems impossible, or simply because they don't know how to attack value- and feeling-based problems. Consider the following two examples.

A housewife-mother decided to seek employment as a way of getting more satisfaction out of life. After a year of working she was just as dissatisfied as before. Why? She wasn't being honest about the source of her dissatisfaction. She didn't like doing the tasks of a housewife and basically found many of the responsibilities of parenthood distasteful. But she hadn't admitted that to herself—or at least had excluded these feelings from her decision to seek employment. The housewife and parent responsibilities wouldn't disappear just because she added an activity. Once she became honest with herself about her feelings, she was prepared to deal directly with the sources of dissatisfaction and arranged to use part of her income to provide for domestic assistance.

A college student who has changed his major four times is about to do it a fifth time. Will his search for a satisfying major end in success? Probably not. This particular student is not being honest with himself regarding his motivation for attending college. It's purely one of personal prestige and parental expectation. He hates studying, and if he were honest with himself he would admit that he would rather work. But by leaving school he might lose the respect of his friends and incur the disfavor of his parents. However, by being honest with himself about his values and concerns, he would open possibilities for solving his dilemma beyond just changing majors.

Failure to be honest with yourself regarding the values and feelings involved in career change is similar to lying to a doctor about your aches and pains. It's difficult to treat a problem if you don't know all the symptoms.

Look Before You Leap

Career change situations frequently occur in which the individual has experienced growing dissatisfaction but has not made a decision to change. Suddenly, a new opportunity occurs and the career change is made. The result may be rewarding. However, we can do ourselves a disservice by not distinguishing between the basic decision to change and the decision to pursue a particular opportunity which arises. The most rational approach to career change is to make the decision to change independent of any particular opportunity for change. Having made that decision, we should then look for alternative opportunities from which to choose. Often, it is difficult to be that rational. The appearance of a particular opportunity can be the deciding persuasive event which tips the scale toward change. Thus we focus on the specific opportunity instead of the more basic issue of the desire to change. When this happens, we still can say to ourselves, "Well, apparently I am ready to make a change. My willingness to pursue this new opportunity tells me that." Thus, to change or not to change is no longer the question. Rather, it becomes "what are other alternatives which might be even more attractive than the one which has just appeared?"

Anticipate the Reaction of Others

Relatively few people live so much alone that their lives do not include relationships with what some call "significant others." Many find the term inadequate, but nevertheless it has some usefulness. Significant others may include spouse, friend, child, parents, lover, boss, student, or coworker. The importance of significant others in regard to career change is three-fold. First, will the anticipated change in your career activities have an impact on them? Will it make them feel sad, happy, or hurt? Will your action reduce their resources or cause them to change their own behavior. These are essentially humanistic concerns.

The second important consideration regarding significant others is your reaction to their reaction. Are *you* going to be sad, unhappy, or hurt because of the manner in which others react to your decision?

The third and most important consideration in regard to the effectiveness of your career change concerns the extent to which you will have to deal with the reactions of significant others. Do you have the skills to deal with them? To illustrate, consider Mrs. A and Mrs. B. They are mothers who have decided to go to work. Mrs. C, an acquaintance of both, raises the question, "But what about your children? Who will fix their breakfasts and see that they get off to school on time?"

Mrs. A replies, "That is a problem. They'll complain, but I'm sure that we can cope with the situation. They can adjust and so can I."

Mrs. B reconsiders; she decides she couldn't live with the guilt she would feel and changes her mind about working. Some will judge Mrs. B as copping out, but that's not fair. Assuming they both know themselves pretty well, each made a valid decision. Mrs. A can deal with the reaction of significant others, and Mrs. B feels that she can't.

One further example to broaden the principle. Mr. D decides he will take up fishing. One effect of this change in his leisure behavior will be his absence from home on some Saturdays and Sundays. Mrs. D has become accustomed to Mr. D's presence on these days, and he anticipates that she will be less than happy with his decision. Mr. D cares for this significant other in his life and in addition wants to avoid dealing with her complaints. He, therefore, makes a point of increasing the non-weekend time in which he participates with Mrs. D. He may not pull it off, but he has followed the guideline of anticipating the reactions of others.

Consider Timing

"Life is essentially a matter of packaging and timing," a wise man once said; and Roger Miller advised us, "Don't change film with a kid on your back!" The principle of timing in regard to career change suggests that important changes are more likely to be successful if they are made one at a time and when the rest of your life is in good shape and running smoothly. It is not always possible to follow this principle. When one gets fired, arrives home to a house in flames, and learns the next day that a sick brother-in-law from Dubuque wants to move in for a couple of months, making one change at a time will not be easy.

The problem of managing several life changes simultaneously can result in none of them being done well. Therefore, go to work and then get a divorce; change jobs and then get married; improve family relationships and then move to the country. **Timing is half of what it's all about.**

CAREER CHANGE COMPETENCIES

In the following pages we will refer to the idea of career change competencies. By acquiring these competencies people can increase the amount of control they have over their lives.

It is true that career change can be precipitated by something that happens to you such as losing a job, physical impairment, flunking out of school, completing school, or loss of a spouse. The more important consideration regarding career change, however, is that it is something which you do, either following some event over which you have little or no control, or because you decide, independent of any forced event, to change. Because career change is done by people and not something done to them, it follows that there are competencies for making a career change.

The career change competencies with which we are concerned consist of skills, concepts, and information. The skills consist of a variety of methods for "making career changes." The concepts provide a means for thinking about your career. Their purpose is to assist in providing some order to the multitude of seemingly chaotic events and circumstances with which most of us must deal from time to time. The importance of the third kind of career change competency, i.e., information, is probably obvious. What many people do not have, however, is an awareness of the many sources of information useful for making career changes.

We have identified eight kinds of career change competencies. Each is described briefly below and will be more thoroughly discussed and illustrated in chapters which follow.

Clarifying Problems. Statements describing career dissatisfaction are often complaints and very general in nature—too general to be of very much use to the career changer. This competency is designed to help clarify those complaints so they become useful information for further steps in the career change process.

Translating Complaints into Career Change Goals. Clearly stated complaints regarding career dissatisfaction are potentially more useful than vague and general complaints. Nevertheless, they are still complaints. Complaints describe "how things are now." They may be informative but provide no basis for action. This competency provides a means for translating complaints into career change goals—statements of "how I would like things to be!"

Increasing Self-Understanding. People differ in regard to the extent to which they accurately understand their values, abilities, and interests. Career changes based on unclear or inaccurate self-understanding are often doomed to failure. These competencies are designed to help you assess and increase your self-understanding.

Dealing with Constraints to Career Change. It is not uncommon to hear people say that they would like to make this or that career change but cannot. Some situation, responsibility, relationship, or lack of resources prevents them from doing so. These reasons for not being able to do what you desire are called constraints. Admittedly, many constraints are real. Many others, however, stem from underlying values and assumptions. When the values and assumptions are examined, we may discover that they have changed without our having realized it. The concepts in this section provide a means for clarifying and dealing with constraints.

Making Career Change Decisions. Career decisions are frequently complex. They often involve clarifying values and goals; identifying alternative means to an end; locating and creating resources; and estimating risks. Competencies regarding these aspects of decision-making are treated in this section.

Implementing Career Change Decisions. Making a decision is one thing; implementing it is another. Competencies described are useful for getting started toward one's new career goals, and keeping at it until the change(s) has been realized.

Making No-Change Career Changes. This is seemingly a contradiction, but actually it is not. Even when major or significant career changes are impossible or have been rejected for some reason, you can often make certain adjustments in your life which can reduce career dissatisfaction and perhaps even bring some increased satisfaction. Several skills for making these adjustments are included in this competency.

Obtaining Career Change Information. Having relevant information about the world of work and nonwork is often a key factor in making an effective career change. Fortunately, a great deal of career change information is readily available. Chapter 9 has annotated lists of several kinds of information regarding career change.

We began this chapter by describing a nontraditional, three-dimensional definition of career. The concept is basic to the materials in the following chapters. Understanding the definition is a prerequisite to learning and using the various career change skills. The following exercise is one means of increasing your understanding of the term career as used in this book.

First reread the career definition from page 16 through 19. Then, in Section A—*Current Situations*—in Table 3, list the activities which describe your current major career activities.

Next, in Section B, labeled *Ideal or Alternative Situations,* list other activities which you believe would be equally or even more satisfying. Define *satisfying* as you please and use your imagination when you list items. Don't worry about being practical at this point. Try to describe what to you would be an ideal career.

Another way to use the table is to complete it for another person and have them complete it for you, each of you estimating how the other perceives his career. Then exchange forms, see how close you came, and explain to each other the basis for your estimates.

TABLE 3. Understanding Your Career

	JOB ACTIVITIES	VOCATION ACTIVITIES	LEISURE ACTIVITIES
Section A Current situations			
Section B Ideal or alternative situations			

chapter 3

Complain
Complain
Complain

Because many people express their career dissatisfactions in the form of complaints, that seems to be a reasonable place to begin our discussion of career change competencies. Complaints, especially vague ones, are not very useful in making changes. Essentially, a complaint describes "how things are now" along with an indication that the complainer doesn't like "the way things are now." Nevertheless, complaints have some use, if only as an indication that one is sufficiently aware of his dissatisfaction to consider doing something about it. More useful, however, would be an indication of "how I would like things to be." The two skills discussed in this chapter are (1) procedures for clarifying what we mean by "things" and (2) translating complaints into goals.

We could, obviously, ignore complaints and begin immediately the business of stating goals. In our experience, however, we have found that this is not as simple as it may seem. People often tend to be much more explicit about what they *don't like,* than about what they *would like.* When that is the case, then it is usually more productive to begin with what we can describe.

CLARIFYING COMPLAINTS

You may be past the point of complaining about your career situation and ready to state career goals. If so, fine. If not, let's begin the task of setting goals by taking a look at your complaints. We will use Table 4 with the remainder of this chapter. Note the categories on the left side under *Conditions.* We have found that most people can describe their career complaints within these five types of conditions. Usually, their complaints refer to some set of existing conditions which are undesirable (I'm bored with my job) or some set of desired conditions which are missing (I wish I was doing something important).

The procedure for using the table begins with a listing of your major career complaints in the *Complaint* column. Note as simply as possible any concerns you have under any of the conditions which apply to you. Complaints might read: I don't make enough money (*Financial*); Henry doesn't pay enough attention to me (*Relationships*); I don't have enough interesting things to do (*Activities*); I'm gloomy much of the time (*Feeling States*); people often mistake my intentions (*Understanding*) .

The next step is to note specific examples of each complaint in the *Examples* column. The key to clarifying complaints is nailing down specific situations or experiences which are causing you dissatisfaction. When you have listed, or tried to list an example for each complaint, then review your two lists and ask yourself questions such as the following: How frequent do these kinds of examples occur? Which are imposed by others and which are your own doing? Are there complaints for which you can't provide examples? What does this mean? Finally, do your complaints place an emphasis on undesirable existing conditions in your life; or is the emphasis on desirable nonexisting conditions? In other words, does your career problem tend to be one of getting away from existing dissatisfying conditions or of creating satisfying conditions. Making this difference clear, if it exists, can be helpful.

An example of this procedure should be valuable. Consider the following. Lucy is a young housewife with two children. She complains of being bored, that housework is dull, of being ignored, and not having any freedom. We asked her to complete the first two columns of the "Career Goals Worksheet" (Table 4). Her complaints and examples are reproduced in Table 5. As you can see, Lucy's general complaints were not very useful in providing direction to a more satisfying career. When she added examples to each complaint, however, she clarified her situation. That is, she pinpointed specific situations or experiences upon which she could concentrate her efforts. She also discovered that her career dissatisfaction was caused by both negative existing conditions and missing desired conditions.

FROM COMPLAINTS TO GOALS

The next task is to translate complaints into career goals. When you were clarifying your complaints in the previous section, you were essentially describing "how things are." In this section, we will attempt to describe "how I would like things to be." Begin by writing a goal in Table 4 for each of the complaints you listed. The following may be helpful.

- **Financial.** Do the desired career changes require money? How much, when, and how soon?

- **Relationships.** Do the desired career changes involve changing the nature of relationships with other people? Initiating new relationships? Breaking off existing ones?

- **Activities.** Do the desired career changes require changing your pattern of activities? In what way? Which activities would be terminated? What are examples of new activities which would be satisfying?

- **Feeling States.** What changes in feelings are involved? What feelings do you want to avoid? Which do you want to experience?

- **Increased Understanding.** Do the career goals involve new learning? What kinds of information are involved? What are examples of situations in which you would use the new understanding? How?

• **Other Conditions.** Do the career change objectives involve any conditions not yet covered? What are they?

We find that many people have difficulty writing goals, so here are three suggestions for writing clear goal statements. First, be sure you make positive statements. Even goals which involve eliminating negative conditions can be stated positively. For example, compare

My goal is to avoid my boss so that misunderstandings will not occur.

with

My goal is to develop a way to communicate more effectively with my boss as a means of resolving hassles when misunderstandings occur.

The first goal statement is narrow, and, even if achieved could bring about other kinds of problems. The second addresses a more basic issue and offers a broader-based solution.

Second, a goal statement should assign the responsibility for change to the person who states the goals. For example, contrast

My goal is to get my wife to participate in my leisure time activities with me.

with

My goal is to identify some leisure activities which my wife and I can enjoy together.

The first example is presumptuous and depends totally upon the wife doing all of the changing to meet the husband's goal. The second is more realistic in that the husband indicates a willingness to do some changing himself in order to meet his own goal.

Third, in many instances it is helpful to specify a time limit by which the goal is to be achieved. Attaching such a limit to goals tends to give them more importance. Goals become more than just wishes or good ideas that we will pursue sometime in the future. When there is some specific point in the future by which you intend to be able to observe the desired change or outcome, you have placed yourself under some pressure to get moving. In addition, if at the specified point in time you have not achieved the goal, there is a built-in signal to reevaluate the goal and the means by which you intend to achieve it. In brief, the most useful statements of career change goals are stated in positive terms, assign responsibility to yourself, and specify a time limit.

After you have written goals for each complaint, list in column 4 a situation or event for each goal which would illustrate that goal being satisfied.

You may be able to think of many examples for each goal, but there is no need to list all of them. The purpose of listing examples for each goal is to provide a test for the realism of your goals. If you cannot think of an example of how a goal could be met, then decide if the goal is really what you mean.

To illustrate the process of translating complaints into goals, we have completed the Lucy example used earlier (Table 6).

TABLE 4. Career Goals Worksheet

CONDITIONS	COMPLAINTS	EXAMPLES
Financial		
Relationships		
Activities		
Feeling states		
Understanding		
Other		

GOALS	EXAMPLES

TABLE 5. Lucy's Career Complaints

CONDITIONS	COMPLAINTS	EXAMPLES
Financial	I haven't any money of my own	–Can't buy a dress or go out to lunch without asking for extra money
Relationships	I'm isolated Husband ignores me	–Seldom talk to adults –Seldom takes me out
Activities	I don't like housework Kids get to me	–Daily cleaning and washing is discouraging –Constant tending to them makes me irritated with husband
Feeling states	I'm depressed often	–Most evenings I'm too discouraged to start an activity –Many mornings I just sit and watch TV
Understanding	I don't know how to change my life	–I waste much time –I don't finish projects
Other		

GOALS	EXAMPLES

TABLE 6. Lucy's Career Goals

CONDITIONS	COMPLAINTS	EXAMPLES
Financial	I haven't any money of my own	–Can't buy a dress or go out to lunch without asking for extra money
Relationships	I'm isolated Husband ignores me	–Seldom talk to adults –Seldom takes me out
Activities	I don't like housework Kids get to me	–Daily cleaning and washing is discouraging –Constant tending to them makes me irritated with husband
Feeling states	I'm depressed often	–Most evenings I'm too discouraged to start an activity –Many mornings I just sit and watch TV
Understanding	I don't know how to change my life	–I waste much time –I don't finish projects
Other		

GOALS	EXAMPLES
–To have spending money of my own	–Go out to lunch once a week –Accumulate a $25 reserve
–To have regular contact with adults –Go out one evening a week with husband	–Shopping with a friend –Garden Club meeting –Movie –Dinner –Visit friends
–To have help with housework and child care	–Help comes in two afternoons a week and I go out
–To feel enthusiasm about myself –To have things to which I look forward	–Getting recognition for what I do from my husband –Some new activity each day
–Learn how to schedule myself	–Making a written plan and staying with it

The following example involving a different set of career change conditions should be instructive.

    Bill is manager of a chain clothing store. He has a variety of outside activities which provide him many personal rewards and satisfactions. The job aspect of his career, in contrast, has become very dissatisfying. He thought he had solved this problem a year ago when he resigned as manager of a chain shoe store and took his present position. We encouraged Bill to complete the Career Complaints Worksheet. His major complaints and examples of each are noted in Table 7.

Bill listed additional sources of dissatisfaction, but these are sufficient to illustrate the point. We asked Bill to review each complaint and the examples he provided. As he reexamined the complaint that employees were generally unreliable, we asked how well they had been informed of the various procedures involved. Specifically, we asked if Joe had been given instructions regarding the inventory procedures; if the "new girl" had been shown how to complete sales slips; and if there was a clear customer refund policy which had been made clear to John.

Bill gave a negative answer to each question and indicated that he just assumed that they would use common sense and follow "correct" procedures. Bill apparently has something to learn about supervision, but that's not our present concern. By using the suggested procedure he was able to discover that one source of career dissatisfaction was much more his own responsibility than he had previously understood.

As he reexamined the examples he listed for the other sources of dissatisfaction he made another important discovery. Bill was reasonably sure that he understood the buying patterns and tastes of his community. He also had been careful to make clear requests for waivers from company policy in each of the examples listed, and to provide reasons. It was to no avail; and this was extremely frustrating. What Bill discovered, or at least clarified, was the importance in his value structure of autonomy and authority to make decisions. He was willing to suffer the consequences of poor decisions, but a job without such authority was likely to be a source of serious career dissatisfaction. When he changed jobs a year ago, he had not given this value much consideration. Now, as he reexamined the former career change situation, he realized that the chief source of dissatisfaction with the former situation was similar to his present circumstances—namely, lack of authority to operate the store according to his judgment.

On the basis of these discoveries Bill translated the complaints into goals, as illustrated in Table 8.

Let us end the chapter by reiterating the suggestion that you put your thoughts on paper. The notion of making notes and lists and filling out forms may appear a bit "Mickey Mouse" to some readers. "That's not necessary," they respond, "I can do it in my head." Perhaps, and if so fine. But to those would-be career changers who have been "doing it in their heads" for some time now without changes occurring, we repeat—try putting it on paper!

Because decision-making begins with goal statements, the Career Goals Worksheet will be useful in Chapter 6 where the topic is decision-making. Sometimes we have so many goals that knowing where to begin is a problem. That issue is dealt with in Chapter 6 also.

TABLE 7. Bill's Career Complaints

CONDITIONS	COMPLAINTS	EXAMPLES
Financial	–Budgetary decisions are made without my consultation	–Last month I was told to drop one employee for budgetary reasons –I don't get to set all my own inventories
Relationships	–Employees are generally unreliable	–Joe failed to complete inventory work –New girl completed sales slip incorrectly –John gave refund without consulting me
Activities	–I have to use company prepared ads, instead of own –Store hours inadequate –I don't have authority to determine inventory levels	–Weekly ads are sent from home office –My request for ad budget denied –Request to open and close later denied –Request for sweaters denied –Request to hold sale on jackets denied
Feeling states	–I feel depressed about my job	–I sometimes dread Mondays and look forward to Fridays
Understanding		
Other		

GOALS	EXAMPLES

TABLE 8. Bill's Career Goals

CONDITIONS	COMPLAINTS	EXAMPLES
Financial	–Budgetary decisions are made without my consultation	–Last month I was told to drop one employee for budgetary reasons –I don't get to set all my own inventories
Relationships	–Employees are generally unreliable	–Joe failed to complete inventory work –New girl completed sales slip incorrectly –John gave refund without consulting me
Activities	–I have to use company prepared ads, instead of my own –Store hours inadequate –I don't have authority to determine inventory levels	–Weekly ads are sent from home office –My request for ad budget denied –Request to open and close later denied –Request for sweaters denied –Request to hold sale on jackets denied
Feeling states	–I feel depressed about my job	–I sometimes dread Mondays and look forward to Fridays
Understanding		
Other		

GOALS	EXAMPLES
–Develop methods to gain more budgetary control from company executives	–Write a position statement –Demonstration of more effective management would be possible if I had control
–Develop in-service training programs and/or orientation meetings for staff	–Monthly meetings with staff on various procedures –Have a system for employee suggestions
–Clarify my point of view with supervisors	–Develop a statement about the advantages and disadvantages of the current policy procedures and distribute it to company executives –Discussion with company executives
–Leave my job worries at work	–Write a list of complaints of the day before I leave work –On the way home think of non-job activities

chapter 4

Know Thyself

What is self-understanding? Essentially it's being able to describe yourself clearly and accurately in regard to characteristics such as values, interests, abilities, and aspirations, and to perceive clearly the various effects you have on other people, and they on you. Self-understanding also involves an appreciation of how you as an individual relate to and are affected by the many groups and institutions within your environment.

Because there are so many dimensions of self and because each of us plays so many roles in a lifetime—many of them simultaneously—acquiring and maintaining an accurate understanding of one's self is a challenging task. It is certainly an enormously important aspect of career development. **Without a fairly clear picture of who you are and what you want your life to be, self direction is almost impossible.** Without self-understanding we tend to react more than act. That can lead to devoting considerable time freeing oneself from unwanted circumstances and situations, many of which could be avoided if we "knew ourself" better in the first place. One who understands himself to a reasonable degree is in a better position to plan, to predict responses to contemplated actions, and to acquire resources and skills required for satisfying career changes.

The following example illustrates the kind of problems which can result from a career change based on inadequate self-understanding. Ralph decided that a divorce would be a solution to many of his problems. However, after three months of living alone, he felt extremely guilty about what he had done to his wife and children. He discovered that a number of his basic values were in conflict with the reality of divorce. For example, he found that he highly valued being able to freely interact with his children and know their daily concerns but was unable to do this under the restrictions of visitation. He discovered that living in a rented apartment was an intolerable situation for him, but saw no way out of the dilemma because of financial constraints.

From an overall view, his values were violated more in his new situation than under the former situation of an unhappy marriage. To achieve some semblance of satisfaction, Ralph would need to change his values and/or learn to cope with an undesirable situation. To have been initially clearer about his values and how they would have been affected by the change would have enabled him to make a more effective change. He could have, among other things, anticipated many negative aspects of a divorce and planned ways of dealing with them had he better understood himself.

You can probably recall situations in which people (perhaps yourself included) became involved in dissatisfying career changes which could have been avoided with greater self-understanding.

There are various means of developing increased self-understanding. One method is through using standardized measures such as aptitude tests and interest and personality inventories. The results of this kind of appraisal, when discussed with a trained professional counselor, can lead to a better understanding of one's self. It is especially helpful to people who have a relatively limited range of career experiences.

Talking to friends can be another useful way to clarify some of your problems. The difficulty is finding someone who is a good listener and capable of asking illuminating questions. Other people increase their self-understanding through self-improvement reading and keeping a diary.

Another means of increasing self-understanding is to review and analyze your past and present experiences. **There is no richer source of information about you than you.** The difficulty is sorting it out. Often you need to rediscover the obvious; view experiences from new perspectives; and discover patterns of life events. The exercises and other materials in the remainder of this chapter have been designed to assist you to review and analyze your past and present experiences. Decide for yourself how much time you want to invest in completing these exercises. Look over the following brief descriptions of the exercise and check those experiences which appeal to you. Each exercise is composed of a brief introduction, a data sheet, and questions to assist in reviewing the information on the data sheet. The exercises need not be completed in any particular order.

The procedure for using the exercises is as follows:

1. Read the brief introduction to the exercise. This will help you understand its purpose and provide you with a mind set for thinking about your experiences.

2. Complete the data sheet for the exercise

3. Use the questions to review the data sheet.

Special Note: One way to increase the value of the exercises is to do them with a partner—a friend, spouse, or someone who wants to increase their own self-understanding. Attempting to clarify your thoughts to another person can be especially enlightening.

Another Special Note: Don't feel that you should complete all of the self-understanding exercises before proceeding to other chapters. While some people find it helpful to complete all of the exercises at this point, many others find it a tedious task. We do suggest, however, that in the process of completing *Career & Life Planning Guide,* you return to this chapter and complete those exercises which seem pertinent to you.

The exercises consist of:

Critical Life Events Grid—Helps to identify important past events relative to career development and may bring out patterns of events and decisions and ways you relate to people. May clarify present goals. Begins on this page.

Values Inventory—Helps you to clarify how your values have changed or stabilized in the past five years. Begins on page 60.

Abilities Inventory—Helps to categorize occupational, personal, and social skills as they relate to career development. Translates educational and social skills into occupational skills. Begins on page 66.

Interest Inventory—Helps you clarify your interests in a number of specific areas. Begins on page 71.

Social Issues—Helps you determine the extent to which your views regarding social issues ought to be considered in career planning. Begins on page 77.

Important Others—Helps you to consider how other people influence your decision making. Begins on page 79.

CRITICAL LIFE EVENTS GRID

One purpose of this exercise is to help you identify past critical events which will have an impact on your career development. The Critical Life Events Grid makes a capsule display of your life to date, and in many instances suggests patterns of decisions and reactions to critical events.

A critical event, as used here, is an experience which you believe to be especially important to you. Examples of critical events could include moving, changing schools, illness, injury, family change, discovering a new interest, getting or losing religion, reading a book, seeing a movie, a journey, or changing occupations.

INSTRUCTIONS: Three age periods have been identified in the first column. Change these or add others so that you have covered your life to date. Try to have each period cover no more than ten years.

Now note critical events in the first row, then the second, and so on, until the grid is complete. You may have no entries for some boxes, and many for others. Be thoughtful and honest.

When you have made all the entries which you think are important, review the grid, asking yourself questions such as:

- Which areas of your life have the most critical events—the fewest?
- What areas are most important?
- What impact have other people had on your development?
- Have your major decisions been effective?
- In making decisions, to what extent do you depend upon advice from others or facts or chance?
- What events would you now have reacted to differently?
- Do you see patterns of events? Is your decision-making pattern the same in different areas of your life?
- How would you like the future to be different from the past?

TABLE 9. Critical Life Events Grid

AGE	SCHOOL	JOB ACTIVITIES	LEISURE ACTIVITIES
1–10			
11–20			
21–30			
31–40			
41–50			
51–60			

NOTE: Reprinted with permission of Charles E. Merrill Publishing Company from *Career Survival Skills* by John W. Loughary and Theresa Ripley. Copyright 1974 by Bell & Howell Company.

PERSONAL CRISES	CAREER THOUGHTS AND ASPIRATIONS	OTHER IMPORTANT EVENTS

TABLE 9.—*Continued*

AGE	PARENTAL INFLUENCE	HEALTH	PEER INFLUENCE
1–10			
11–20			
21–30			
31–40			
41–50			
51–60			

SIGNIFICANT OTHERS INFLUENCE (TEACHERS, RELATIVES, CHILDREN, SPOUSE)	MAIN PHILOSOPHY, BELIEFS, AND CONCERNS

VALUES

Many people experience a change in values in midlife. This is understandable. Often times a number of events are occurring simultaneously. For example, the children are older; the job may be monotonous; and relationships may be changing.

This exercise is concerned with understanding and being able to describe your value system. It is not concerned with judging those values. From our point of view, it is impossible to label a value as good or bad but it is often possible to identify values which the majority of people accept or reject. For example, you might place a positive value upon a couple living together without being married, but society, in general, places a negative value on this. To hold this value you must be willing to contend with society's reaction.

One other point about values. Frequently we encounter situations in which two or more values are in conflict. In such cases any course of action will result in violating a particular value. For example, suppose Jane, a 36-year-old wife and mother of two teenagers, discovers she is pregnant. She is very distressed because as she had projected her career her childbearing and caring days were past. She places great value on her job and the freedom to pursue her many interests. An obvious solution and one acceptable to her is abortion. However, her husband is strongly opposed to abortion. Because she also values her husband's respect, she foresees a serious dilemma. Having the abortion would violate his values, and continuing the pregnancy and bearing the child will violate her values of personal freedom.

Resolving value conflicts is by no means an easy task. However, a clear understanding of your own value system can often provide the basis for determining the relative importance of conflicting values.

INSTRUCTIONS: In the following five tables five value areas have been chosen for examination. After reading each definition, use the space provided to describe your current values in that area and your values five years ago.

When you have completed all the tables, consider the following:

- Rank the five value areas in order of importance to you, both as of now and as of five years ago. Compare the two rankings.

- If you have had some changes in values, what caused the changes?

- Do you think you will change your values significantly in the next five years in any of the five value areas? Why or why not?

- Do you hold values which are inconsistent with your present situation?

- What impact do your values have for making career changes?

Table 10.—SOCIAL AND MORAL VALUES: Consider your current and past reactions to such issues as abortion, premarital sex, marriage, racial and sexual prejudice and discrimination, ecological concerns, and urban vs. rural living. List moral and social concerns that have been of particular importance in your thinking and development.

TABLE 10. Social and Moral Values

CURRENT VALUES	VALUES FIVE YEARS AGO

Table 11.—POLITICAL VALUES: Recent national and international political events have caused many people to examine their political opinions and attitudes. Describe both your past and current political orientation; if there has been a change, note what event(s) caused the change.

TABLE 11. Political Values

CURRENT VALUES	VALUES FIVE YEARS AGO

Table 12.—RELIGIOUS VALUES: Some people find "religion" as they get older and others lose it. Summarize your thinking about personal beliefs and concerns regarding religion, and list them for the two time periods.

TABLE 12. Religious Values

CURRENT VALUES	VALUES FIVE YEARS AGO

Table 13.—ECONOMIC/MATERIAL VALUES: Describe what you believed to be essential for "the good life" five years ago contrasted with your current thinking. Compare the material goods needed for each lifestyle.

TABLE 13. Economic/Material Values

CURRENT VALUES	VALUES FIVE YEARS AGO

Table 14.—AESTHETIC VALUES: What did you find aesthetically pleasing five years ago vs. today (e.g., art/painting, films, nature, jewelry, athletic skill). Describe the need for aesthetic things in your life five years ago and today.

TABLE 14. Artistic Values

CURRENT VALUES	VALUES FIVE YEARS AGO

ABILITIES

For many people, abilities or skills is the critical concern regarding career changes. This exercise provides a means of conceptualizing past experiences with an emphasis on the abilities and skills which you demonstrated in those experiences. A special note is in order to those who have had little or no "paid work" experiences and who immediately conclude that they are without career skills. That is most likely nonsense. **Everybody's done something!**

The less formal kinds of abilities are at least equally and often more important to career development than those learned in school. By definition, half of the people in school are below average with regard to any ability measured, and the marking and grade reporting procedures used by schools consistently points this out to those "under average." The tragedy is that the standards which schools use to measure academic abilities often have little relationship to job requirements. In other words, the majority of people who are "below average" in academic skills such as reading, writing, and calculating can do very well in the majority of jobs available to them. The problem which our schools perpetrate in regard to abilities and career development is that they don't measure the more relevant abilities, and what they do measure is done inappropriately. So take heed! You probably have much more going for you than you think. In the process of getting to this point in your life, you have probably demonstrated that you can talk, think, resolve conflicts, solve problems, add, divide, read, and explain, to name only a few abilities. You may not have thought of these as career skills, but they are. Thus, don't prejudge yourself.

The first part of the exercise consists of an inventory of your past experiences. The second part of the exercise helps you translate experiences into abilities.

INSTRUCTIONS: Part I. Briefly describe five successful and five unsuccessful experiences you have had in each of the four areas below. Suggestions for each of the four areas are:

> *Work Experiences*—list successful and unsuccessful aspects of paid and nonpaid work experiences you have had.
>
> *School Experiences*—list specific academic classes in which you have succeeded and list those in which you have not succeeded.
>
> *Voluntary and Leisure Experiences*—list activities (clubs, sports, hobbies) in which you have participated that were successful and list those that were not successful.

Relationship Experiences—list specific experiences you can recall in which you felt you were successful in understanding the feelings of another (or group) or helped an individual or group resolve a problem. List experiences in which you were not successful in doing this.

After completing the form, think about or better yet share Part I of the inventory and give a brief description of each experience listed. Note what made the experience successful or unsuccessful. Focus as much as possible on the skills and abilities that were utilized in each experience, and how these abilities and skills affected the success or nonsuccess of the experience.

Utilizing the information from Part I, complete Part II of the inventory individually.

Part II. Each space in Column 1 lists a different kind of ability. Beginning with the first ability (managing/organizing), note in Column 2 those responses requested. Do the same for each row.

After completing Part II, discuss your listing. Consider the following:

- Have you overlooked some abilities?
- Have you rated your abilities correctly? That is, are you underrating or overrating yourself?
- What abilities would you like to add to your repertoire?

TABLE 15. Inventory of Abilities—Part I

PAID AND NONPAID WORK EXPERIENCES	SCHOOL EXPERIENCES
Successful	Successful
1.	1.
2.	2.
3.	3.
4.	4.
5.	5.
Unsuccessful	Unsuccessful
1.	1.
2.	2.
3.	3.
4.	4.
5.	5.

LEISURE EXPERIENCES	HUMAN RELATIONSHIP EXPERIENCES
Successful 1. 2. 3. 4. 5.	Successful 1. 2. 3. 4. 5.
Unsuccessful 1. 2. 3. 4. 5.	Unsuccessful 1. 2. 3. 4. 5.

TABLE 16. Inventory of Abilities—Part II

ABILITY	EXPERIENCE DEMONSTRATING I HAVE THE ABILITY	EXPERIENCE DEMONSTRATING I DO NOT HAVE THE ABILITY	MY ABILITY LEVEL IN THIS AREA IS:				
			Very High	High	Average	Fair	Poor
Managing/ organizing							
Oral communication							
Written communication							
Supervising							
Planning							
Working under pressure							
Leadership							
Following instructions							
Technical skills							
Personal relations							
Other skills not covered— specify							

INTERESTS

Interest is defined as "a feeling of curiosity, fascination, or absorption." As a child, you might have been fascinated by firefighters, absorbed in your stamp collection, and curious about the old house in the neighborhood that had so many ghost stories told about it. All of these things were of interest to you. Thus, when someone asked you "What would you like to be when you grow up?" your response—depending on your current interest—might have been firefighter, philatelist, or detective. Your response was primarily based on your interests. As you grew older, considerations such as difficulty of work and amount of income began to temper your interests.

Nevertheless, interests remain a very critical aspect of career change. One important criteria in selecting career activities, therefore, is whether it satisfies some of your interests.

The exercise that follows encourages you to consider how you feel about twenty specific interest areas. Use the exercise to structure your thinking about your past, current, and predicted interests as well as relating those interests to specific career choices. There are two parts to the exercise. Complete Part I of the "Interest Inventory" (Table 17) now.

INSTRUCTIONS: Part I. Listed on pages 72–75 are twenty kinds of career activities in which you may or may not be interested. For each activity list five words that describe your feelings about it. For example, if you enjoy public speaking you might list exciting, challenging, stimulating, fun, and proud. On the other hand if you are fairly nervous before speaking in public and are not praised for your efforts, you might list scary, nerve-racking, embarrassed, nervous, and fearful. For those areas in which you have not had experience, use your imagination to estimate how you might react to the activity. Ignore the circles and short lines.

TABLE 17. Interest Inventory—Part I

Public speaking

_____ _____

_____ _____

_____ _____

_____ _____

_____ _____

Total Score ◯

Science

_____ _____

_____ _____

_____ _____

_____ _____

_____ _____

Total Score ◯

Direct sales

_____ _____

_____ _____

_____ _____

_____ _____

_____ _____

Total Score ◯

Management

_____ _____

_____ _____

_____ _____

_____ _____

_____ _____

Total Score ◯

Marketing

_____ _____

_____ _____

_____ _____

_____ _____

_____ _____

Total Score ◯

Military activities

_____ _____

_____ _____

_____ _____

_____ _____

_____ _____

Total Score ◯

Supervision

_____ ___

_____ ___

_____ ___

_____ ___

_____ ___

Total Score ◯

Teaching

_____ ___

_____ ___

_____ ___

_____ ___

_____ ___

Total Score ◯

Agriculture

_____ ___

_____ ___

_____ ___

_____ ___

_____ ___

Total Score ◯

Recreational leadership

_____ ___

_____ ___

_____ ___

_____ ___

_____ ___

Total Score ◯

Medical service

_____ ___

_____ ___

_____ ___

_____ ___

_____ ___

Total Score ◯

Social service

_____ ___

_____ ___

_____ ___

_____ ___

_____ ___

Total Score ◯

TABLE 17.—*Continued*

Art/Music/Drama

_____ _____

_____ _____

_____ _____

_____ _____

_____ _____

Total Score ◯

Homemaking

_____ ___

_____ ___

_____ ___

_____ ___

_____ ___

Total Score ◯

Outdoor

_____ ___

_____ ___

_____ ___

_____ ___

_____ ___

Total Score ◯

Organizational
activities

_____ ___

_____ ___

_____ ___

_____ ___

Total Score ◯

Religious
activities

_____ ___

_____ ___

_____ ___

_____ ___

Total Score ◯

Numerical work

_____ ___

_____ ___

_____ ___

_____ ___

Total Score ◯

Mechanical   Planning

_____ ____   _____ ____
_____ ____   _____ ____
_____ ____   _____ ____
_____ ____   _____ ____
_____ ____   _____ ____

Total Score   ◯   Total Score   ◯

Now, indicate in the table whether each word you listed has a positive, negative, or neutral connotation to you. Score each response as follows: positive = +1; negative = −1; neutral = 0. Derive the total score for each area. The following is an example.

Public Speaking
  Being sought after   *0*
  Challenging   *+1*
  Rewarding   *+1*
  Time-consuming   *−1*
  Draining   *−1*

Total Score   ◯

INSTRUCTIONS: Part II: In Table 18 list those areas that had a total score of +2 or above under Positive Areas and those that had —2 or below scores under Negative Areas. List the remainder under Neutral Areas.

Review both parts of the inventory. Consider and discuss the following:

- What experiences have you had in each area that account for your positive or negative statements?
- Why might you anticipate dramatic changes in your interests in any of these areas?
- Were you surprised by any of the scores? Why?
- How might you use this information about your interests?
- Were there some areas in which you had no experience? If so, how were the words selected—societal stereotypes, peer discussions, secondhand experiences?
- How might you gain experience in areas in which you had no experience to determine whether your predicted interests would hold up?

TABLE 18. Interest Inventory—Part II

POSITIVE AREAS	NEGATIVE AREAS	NEUTRAL AREAS

SOCIAL ISSUES

Current local, national, and international events affect each of us in different ways. For example, in 1970 the environment and ecology movement was just beginning to emerge as an important national issue. The public was bombarded with facts, theories, scare stories, and testimonials concerning the movement and the problems associated with the environment. The public responded in many different ways—from making a concerted effort to recycle products to choosing ecology/environmental science as a major in college. It was difficult not to respond to the movement even if your response was resentment toward all the time and energy being expended just talking about it. Consider another example, the assassination of President John F. Kennedy. How did you react? Was it anger, hurt, sadness, resignation? Some people reacted by deciding to work in a political organization that they felt could have a desirable impact. Both of these examples illustrate how societal issues and trends do have an effect on individual career development.

Consider another kind of social issue which can have a direct bearing on individual career development. **Many men do not believe that the changing roles of women have much effect on them.** It does, though, in very specific ways. First of all, equal opportunity for the sexes is, in many instances, being legislated. Thus, women have the legal right to apply for positions that have formerly been male-dominated, such as telephone lineperson, mechanic, or traveling salesperson. Conversely, more men are being considered as secretaries, elementary school teachers, and medical technicians. Affirmative action also affects males. By affirmative action an employer means that if a male and a female applicant are competing for a position, it is highly likely that they will employ the female and upgrade her skills if necessary.

This exercise helps you consider the impact which selected current social issues might have on your career development. The first step is to complete Table 19, the "Impact of Social Issues" data sheet.

INSTRUCTIONS: Several current social trends and issues are listed in the first column. In the second column briefly describe what you believe to be the most important aspect of each social issue. In the third column identify specific ways in which the issue affects your current behavior. Do the same for each issue listed. After completing the form, share the contents of the table issue by issue. Then discuss the following questions:

- In the next five years what social trend or issue do you predict will most influence your behavior?
- How do you think social issues influenced your parents' career development?

TABLE 19. Impact of Social Issues

SOCIAL TREND OR ISSUE	IMPORTANT ASPECTS OF SOCIAL TREND	IMPACT OF ISSUE ON MY BEHAVIOR
Changing roles of men and women		
Racial and ethnic prejudice and discrimination		
Ecology, energy crisis, and overpopulation		
National leadership		
Unemployment and job availability		
Marriage and divorce trends		
Inflation		
International relations		
(Your own choice— specify another social issue)		

IMPORTANT OTHERS

Each of us is influenced by other people. The degree of influence varies from situation to situation and by our individual intellectual and emotional makeup. Regardless of our desire for independence, there are few people, if any, who aren't influenced significantly by the actions of or concern for other people who are important to them. That in part is what we mean by "important others." For example, some people are highly influenced by their marriage partner; their spouse directly or indirectly selects their social activities, determines their financial commitments, and decides the number of children they will have. On the other extreme are couples who each maintain relatively independent personal and professional lives. Some place in the middle are couples who acknowledge that they influence each other but attempt to allow for the optimal freedom of each. Because being influenced by others is inevitable, it is important to understand how this influence affects your career decisions.

The influence of others can go unnoticed, either because of the subtle ways in which people convey their desires or because we become so accustomed to long-standing values and behavior patterns that we forget that they exist, or assume that they remain valid. How many times, for example, have you resisted doing some desired action because you assumed that someone would think badly of you? In such situations, how often do you check your assumptions? Would they really be upset? Why? For how long? Perhaps an even more important question in such situations is the question, "So what?" Given that some person important to you disagrees with your plans or aspirations, what is the worst possible thing that could happen to you—or them—if you proceed? Sometimes the answer underscores the importance of the other person to us, and other times it points up the irrationality of our thinking. In any case it usually clarifies the influence that another has on our own behavior and this enhances our decision-making efforts.

Let it be clear that being influenced by others is not necessarily good or bad. **Life would be less rewarding without concerns for others, and careers would be shallow.** On the other hand, constant deference to the wishes and priorities of other people can lead to a life of frustration and unhappiness and to careers which are flat. The point is to maximize control over your destiny by understanding who influences your behavior and deciding the extent to which that influence is acceptable to you.

Table 20 provides a basis for deciding who usually influences your life and in what areas. Completing it can provide a basis for reassessing the extent to which you want others to influence your career decisions.

INSTRUCTIONS: Seven decision-making areas are listed in the first column. In the second column list people in your life who influence(d) you in each decision-making area. In the third column, opposite the name of each person listed, use the following point scale to rate the degree of influence of each person: (1) very high; (2) high; (3) average; (4) low; (5) negligible.

After completing the form, share the contents of the table and discuss which people seem to influence you the most. Rank these people from most to least influence in the spaces below.

1.
2.
3.
4.
5.
6.
7.
8.
9.
10.

- Are you surprised at the results?
- Do you see yourself as more or less independent than you thought?
- In what areas would you like to have more influence from other people? In which areas would you like to have less?
- Reverse roles. Which people do you influence and how? Would you like to change that?

TABLE 20. Persons and Areas of Influence

DECISION-MAKING AREAS	INFLUENTIAL OTHERS	DEGREE OF INFLUENCE
Mate selection		
Educational decisions		
Social behavior		
Choice of number of children		
Entertainment selection		
Job choices		
Financial spending habits		

USING YOUR SELF-UNDERSTANDING

If you have completed all or some of the previous exercises (tables), either you know some facts you did not know or you confirmed what you already knew. Perhaps you saw facts and perceptions in a different light so that an "aha" response occurred. Sometimes by viewing incidents in a different structure or arrangement they can have a new meaning.

If you want a quick indication of what you have learned about yourself try the following: Review your data sheets from the tables and note the answer to the following question regarding each. What is the most important discovery you made about yourself regarding Critical Life Events, Abilities, Values, Interests, Social Issues, Important Others?

So, how can you use your self-understanding? First, it can be used—in fact it will be a necessity—in reading the remainder of this book. We will be continually urging you to use your self-understanding in considering career changes. This will be an active process and involve more than just "reading the book." You will be encouraged to examine many of your assumptions and perceptions. The result should be that your self-understanding should be even clearer and sharper at the end of the book than it is now.

A second way to utilize increased self-understanding is in making day-to-day decisions. That is, don't reserve your increased awareness only for those times that major decisions are to be made. For example, if after completing the Abilities Inventory (Tables 15 and 16), you listed a number of specific examples which demonstrate you do not work well under pressure, use that knowledge in everyday circumstances. The message is clear—use your self-understanding profitably and it can reap benefits.

chapter 5

I Can't Change Because...

When we do career counseling, people frequently tell us about their constraints—those circumstances which prohibit them from making career changes. Constraint statements take the form of "I can't do that because . . . ." Career change constraints are obstacles between your present situation and the career change goal you want to reach.

In this chapter we will examine career change constraints and illustrate several means of clarifying constraint statements. The last section of the chapter gives a specific procedure for analyzing constraints.

Our basic contention is that many career change constraints are more a result of careless use of language and unclear values and assumptions than of any actual circumstances which prohibit us from doing what we desire.

The imprecise or careless use of language can result in what appears to be unchangeable constraints. One language trap frequently encountered is confusing the impossible with the improbable. We often describe constraints as absolutes, when in fact they are not. We speak in such a manner to suggest that some set of fixed, unchangeable, unavoidable circumstances has predetermined our destiny—or at least placed permanent limitations on it. Some constraints, of course, are absolute.

If, for example, your goal is to enter officer's candidate school and you are forty-five years old, your age is an absolute constraint. Or, if you have 20/200 vision and aspire to be a commercial pilot, your vision is an absolute constraint. If, on the other hand, you are a married woman responsible for raising a family and your goal is to graduate from college, your family responsibilities do not constitute an absolute constraint to your career goal. They may and probably do make attending college improbable, but not impossible. There are various things you can do to overcome the constraint if you so decide. Obviously, you can also decide not to overcome the constraint. Consider the following two examples in which absolute constraints are a function of the language of the speaker, not outside circumstances.

I can't play basketball because I am a paraplegic.

Most of us would acknowledge that that statement is generally accurate. But it is also untrue. It refers to an impossible event, that of any paraplegic ever playing basketball. What the speaker probably means by that statement is:

Most paraplegics don't play basketball,

which is a true statement. A paraplegic playing basketball is an improbable event, but some paraplegics do participate in that sport. Several gather each year to play in an international paraplegic basketball tournament. To most people the inaccuracy of the statement is of little or no concern. The imprecise language isn't important. To a few people, however, namely paraplegics who would like to play basketball, the imprecise language has serious consequences.

A blind man once said, "I'll never be able to read newsprint." With that statement he imposed an absolute constraint on his career development. It is accurate to say that most blind people don't read newsprint, but it is not true that all don't. There are available at least two instruments which enable blind people to read print. One is tactile, the other audio.

Another way of examining constraints resulting from the careless use of language is to look for implicit predictions. Take, for example, the dissatisfied housewife who stated,

> I can't go to work because my family would never allow it.

Now, obviously, it is not true that she can't go to work. It could be a difficult career change, but women who are housewives obtain outside employment every day. The career change could be difficult for many reasons—but not impossible. What about her prediction that "my family would never allow it"? Would they lock her in the basement? Chain her to the bed? We don't think so. In the real sense of "allow" she is ultimately responsible only to herself. She may be correct in predicting that her family might object, argue, pout, or carry on in any number of ways aimed at getting her to change her mind about going to work. She can also predict that dealing with their objections might even be unpleasant. But that is a very different kind of constraint than someone having total control over her actions.

Another means of clarifying constraints which we state as absolutes is to look for words such as "all," "never," "can't," "none," "impossible," "every," and "only." We often use such words carelessly. To return to our starting point, we often state something to be impossible, when in fact it is only improbable.

You may think, sure, you've got a point. But for all practical purposes many things which are improbable might just as well be impossible. We would agree. But only if you let us add that "for all practical purposes anything which is not impossible is also probable." This is no Horatio Alger power-of-positive-thinking stance we are taking. We are simply suggesting that many times we are careless with language and in the process convince ourselves that something is impossible when it is only improbable. If it is improbable, then by definition it also has some possibility of occurring. The more clearly we understand and describe the situations with which we are dealing and the variables involved, the more likely we will discover constraints which are in large part really language problems.

In our everyday use of language most of us use a kind of verbal short-hand. When we make statements such as "I'm going shopping," "I'm going to clean house," "Please prepare the Smith contract," or "I enjoyed the party," we are using shorthand. The words shopping, cleaning, prepare, and enjoy as used in these statements each refer to a large number of specific events. Most of the time verbal shorthand is effective. In fact, we probably all know a few people who ought to make more use of it!

With regard to describing constraints, however, verbal shorthand can cause problems. In order to deal with constraints it is important to understand the specific issues involved. A constraint which appears to be absolute when stated in general terms, may be relatively easy to overcome when we become specific about what actually is involved. As an aid in being specific we have identified four types of constraints which often stand in the way of career change. These are *financial, skills, emotional,* and *management* constraints, respectively. One or more can be part of a career change problem. These often overlap, and certainly other ways of classifying constraints could be devised. These four, however, will serve our purpose.

Before examining the advantages of being specific about each of these four kinds of constraints, it should be helpful to consider the example of Bill who stated, "I want to take the new job offer but I can't. My wife won't let me."

Having read the foregoing statement, you are already one step ahead of Bill and are asking him if he really means to say that his wife has some absolute power over what he does? He sheepishly admits that she doesn't. What he means, he says, is that "If I took the new job there would be hell to pay with Martha." Aha! A much more precise statement. Well, at least he's no longer talking in absolutes.

"What would be the nature of Martha's reactions?" you ask.

"Well," Bill replies, "first of all the job pays less than the one I have now and she's worried about being able to meet our family expenses."

"Anything else?," you inquire.

"Yeah. The new job involves a lot of traveling. Martha doesn't drive, so she'd be stuck at home. Also, she thinks that with my being gone she would have problems managing the kids and all the other family concerns. Just 'too much to do,' she says."

"And what do *you* think?," you ask Bill.

"Ah, all those things could be worked out. My concern is the hassles and bad feelings that could develop between Martha and me as we tried to work them out! We'd both be upset."

Congratulations! You've helped Bill come a long way. He's moved from making an absolute constraint statement to describing four kinds of relatively specific constraints with which he and his family would have to deal in order to make a satisfying career change. In short Bill has described:

- a *financial* constraint—the need to exist for a period of time with a reduced salary;
- a *skill* constraint—the problem of increasing Martha's mobility;
- a *management* constraint—the problem of providing Martha with help in family management;
- an *emotional* constraint—the need to deal with bad feelings between Martha and himself.

That's coming a long way from "paying hell to Martha."

Being specific about constraints is not always as easy to do as it may seem. Because of that we will discuss briefly each of the four types of constraints.

Financial

Financial or finance-related constraints are often relatively obvious. When we indicate that a particular career change can't be made because of insufficient funds, there is not much question about what is meant. Nevertheless, being more specific about financial constraints can lead to finding means of overcoming them. For example, when Gloria, a pre-medical student, concluded, "I can't go to medical school because it costs too much," there was little she could do about her plight. When, however, she became more specific about this general constraint and said to herself, "If I go to medical school then I will need to obtain about $10,000 for tuition and living expenses," she significantly changed the nature of what she could do about the constraint. When she became even more specific and said, "If I go to medical school, then I will have to generate $350 for living expenses each month for four years and a tuition and book payment of $350 for each of twelve terms," she developed a perception of her constraint which allowed her to pursue various means of dealing with it. She didn't need all of the money at once, and she was more likely to see that multiple sources of funds could be pursued. In other words, it is probably true that she cannot go out tomorrow and put her hands on $10,000. However, the probability of obtaining the same amount over a four-year period by using a multiple-funding plan (e.g., loans, scholarships, and summer jobs) may be high enough to make pursuing medical school a reasonable goal. On the other hand, from the perspective and values of a given person, pursuing such a goal may be unattractive. In either case, however, the decision is based on what we are willing to do and to risk, and not on some constraint attributed to conditions beyond our control.

There are, of course, financial constraints beyond the control of most of us. What we are suggesting is that poorly stated financial constraints frequently cause people to forfeit the career change game before they have an opportunity to play it.

Skills

"I cannot get a job," states the middle-aged woman whose children are all in school, "because I don't have any work skills." As we pointed out in Chapter 4, people frequently define their skills in a manner which inhibits desired career change. If Mrs. Middle-Age were to take tests in typing, shorthand, bookkeeping, truck driving, or any other activity for which she lacks training or experience, we could predict fairly accurately that she would score low. In regard to those kinds of skills, she's absolutely correct. She has none. However, if we could test her on such skills as communications, human relations, dealing with angry children and an upset husband, planning, shopping, predicting the desires of others, and organizing, we would have no basis for such a negative prediction. She may well have acquired these skills during the course of her homemaker career experience.

People differ in regard to the extent to which they develop the kinds of skills just noted, but it is unlikely that anyone can live part of their life without developing some useful abilities which can be regarded as career-related skills. To the extent that is true, then most people have some skills which can facilitate career change.

Acquiring new skills is a subject discussed in Chapter 7. **There are increasing opportunities to learn new skills, both occupational-specific and those with more general application.** Community colleges, adult education programs, and retirement centers, for example, offer instruction in everything from apron-making to Zen, and often at little cost. The most effective and satisfying use of such skill development resources can be made when present skills have been analyzed and career change objectives defined.

Emotional

Emotional constraints may be less amenable to the kind of straight-forward analysis suggested for financial and skills constraints, but neverthe-less, they can often be clarified to some useful extent. Emotional career change constraints are those which refer to feelings which you would experi-ence or need to deal with if career changes were made. "I can't get a divorce because I couldn't stand the guilt I would feel," and "I can't change jobs because I would be too nervous and anxious about succeeding in the new one" are examples of emotional constraint statements. It is difficult to predict whether the anticipated emotion would be as debilitating as you imagine, but even so, clarification is often possible. Consider the second of the two examples just given. We can ask such questions as, "What do you mean by 'nervous and anxious'? What form does it take in your behavior? What are examples of situations where being nervous and anxious got in the way of doing what you wanted to do? How did you deal with your anxiety in these situations? What were the effects of your efforts to deal with them? What was the 'thing' in each of these situations which made you nervous? Looking back over these situations, would you now react differently? How?" Answers to these and similar questions should produce a specific and useful definition of being "nervous and anxious." For example, we may now know that anxious and nervous means in part "sweaty hands, less speech fluency, bluntness with people, and decreased ability to understand and follow a supervisor's instructions." If so, we can now translate the constraint,

I can't change jobs because I would be so nervous and anxious about succeeding in the new one,

to the statement,

If I am to succeed at the new job, then I will have to deal with such things as sweaty hands, decreased speech fluency, being blunt with people, and misunderstanding instructions.

Chapter 7, "Making a Difference," describes a variety of procedures that can be useful in dealing with emotional constraints. These include, for example, practicing the desired behavior in a safe situation before encountering it in the "real" situation; establishing reward schemes for doing the desired behavior; and verbal (talking to yourself) methods of achieving greater self-control.

The example we have been using provides a further illustration of a means of gaining a clearer understanding of an emotional constraint and determining how we might deal with it. We can perform the kind of analysis just illustrated on the term "succeeding." The term, depending upon the individual, can mean anything from "not being fired" to "becoming president of the company." In this example, an accurate definition of what is acceptable as "succeeding" may help reduce the anxious behavior. If, in other words, you have realistic aspirations and can define the conditions or circumstances which would exist when these aspirations were being met, then you have a means for assessing success. Without this kind of definition, the person who anticipates being nervous and anxious about "succeeding" (whatever that means) will probably see his predictions come true. **If we don't know where we want to go, it's impossible to know when we get there.**

Management

Examples of management constraints are "I can't accept the committee chairwomanship because the house and kids would fall apart," and "I can't accept the promotion to district manager which involves considerable travel, because my wife would be overburdened with managing the children."

Management constraints are different from emotional constraints in that they are not emotional experiences or situations that one fears, but rather the inability or unwillingness to deal with complexities that a career change might cause.

As with the three previous kinds of constraints, management constraints may be sufficiently powerful for deciding to abandon the contemplated career change. However, an analysis similar to those described for other kinds of constraints can often lead to a much clearer definition of the management problems involved, thus providing a basis for deciding whether we can or want to deal with them.

ANALYZING CONSTRAINTS

Up to this point we have urged you to (1) determine whether constraints are absolute or relative; (2) be careful with the language you use to describe constraints to yourself; and (3) be specific about what a constraint involves. In this section we will describe a specific method for analyzing constraints, once you have them clearly in mind. The procedure involves changing a *constraint statement* to a *contingency statement*. You will remember that a constraint statement takes the form "I can't change because of 'something.'" A contingency statement simply indicates what must be done about the constraint if you are to make the change. It takes the form, "If I change, then I will have to deal with 'something.'" Instead of viewing the "something" as an absolute obstacle to a career change, we concentrate on dealing with it so we can reach our goal. Reaching the goal, then, becomes contingent upon our dealing effectively with the "something."

The procedure is based on the idea that many constraint statements entail one or more underlying values or assumptions. Often the values and assumptions are not clear to us, and sometimes we feel less strong about a value than we have assumed. The procedure for analyzing constraints is to determine whether an underlying value or assumption is present and to clarify it if it does exist. The procedure involves the following four steps:

• Make a *constraint statement* using the form "I cannot do A because of B."

- Identify and state *underlying value(s) or assumption(s)* if they exist.
- Analyze and *clarify* the value or assumption.
- Make a *contingency statement* using the form "If I do A, then I must ____."

In short, the process is one of determining whether an "I can't do A because of B . . ." statement can be changed to an "If I do A, then I will have to deal with B" statement. Consider the following illustrations of the procedure:

Constraint Statement: I cannot attend evening classes because I have small children for whom I must care.

Underlying Assumption: Something undesirable will happen to my children either now or in their long-term development if I do not personally supervise them every evening.

Clarification: That's foolish. I can obtain an adequate baby-sitter and pursue my own interests which shouldn't be ignored.

Contingency Statement: If I am to attend night classes, then I will need to arrange for responsible child care for my children.

Constraint Statement: I cannot resign as district sales manager and take a less demanding, lower paying job in a small town because of the cost of maintaining my family.

Underlying Value: My present standard of living is the minimum I will voluntarily accept. Whatever the advantages of small town living, they don't compensate for a reduced income level.

Clarification: That's probably not true, or I wouldn't be considering the change in the first place. We have many luxuries, some of which don't seem to provide much pleasure.

Contingency Statement: If I change my occupation and move from the city, then I will need to reduce family costs such as the second car, high entertainment expenses, and expensive vacations.

Constraint Statement: I cannot take a part-time job which would give me time to pursue my writing interests because we need money for the children's college education.

Underlying Value: It is my responsibility as a parent to finance a college education for my children.

Clarification: I held this value years ago, but question it now. The availability of a low-cost community college presents a viable option to sending them away to college. That may not be as much to their liking, but they too can adjust.

Contingency Statement: If I reduce my income the children will need to find means of paying for their college education.

Constraint Statement: I cannot devote more time to service club work because my spouse would resent it.

Underlying Assumption: The satisfaction derived from club work would not compensate for the unpleasant relationship with my spouse.

Clarification: That's true. However, I could probably find means of appeasing him.

Contingency Statement: If I devote more time to service club work, then I will need to anticipate complaints and engage in compensatory activities to maintain good relationships with spouse.

These examples illustrate that about the only response we can make to an initial constraint statement is to agree that "If you say you can't, then I guess you can't." But, as the examples point out, identifying the underlying values or assumptions may lead to a revised statement. What frequently occurs is that we are able to change an absolute statement (I cannot) to a description of the conditions which would need to prevail in order for us to take the action.

It is true that such conditions often can be severe, either regarding our ability to bring them about or because of some value conflict. For example, consider a couple who would like to shuck their jobs and open a small business. They have decided that this is not possible due to financial constraints.

Constraint Statement: We cannot go into business for ourselves because we lack sufficient capital.

Underlying Value: Our savings were hard to come by and economic risk is to be avoided.

Clarification: We are not willing to risk our savings and go in debt in order to start a business which has no guarantee of being successful.

Contingency Statement: If we start a small business, then we will have to risk our savings and accept the responsibility of repaying a loan even if the business fails.

The couple may still decide not to open the small business, but two aspects of the situation have changed. First, they are no longer placing the blame for their not taking a desired action on some externally imposed constraint. Instead, they have recognized that the desired action is possible, but that they themselves may be unwilling to risk their savings and future earnings. Second, they have moved from thinking in terms of absolutes toward thinking in terms of alternatives. Having begun this kind of analysis they are more likely to examine what they mean by "starting a small business." They may have been assuming that this would require both of their efforts on a full-time basis. They may now discover other options such as beginning on a smaller scale with one or both continuing some outside employment, or selecting a business which initially can be operated weekends and evenings.

Career change constraints which involve personal obligations and relationships are perhaps the most difficult to analyze. Dealing with such constraints usually cannot be done unilaterally. We may believe that others involved in the relationship or obligation must be consulted, and further, that the others' perceptions of the relationship or obligation may not be clear or that they differ from our own perception. Analyzing and clarifying these kinds of constraints may involve considerable negotiation, which in itself may represent a potential threat to the relationship. A typical example involves a husband who is contemplating a job change which would mean uprooting his family and moving them to a new community. He predicts that even raising this constraint for discussion with his wife and children may be so upsetting to them that they would be anxious for months to come. Nevertheless, it is impossible to clarify the strength of the constraint without consulting those involved in it. There is no easy solution.

One means of approaching other people involved in an emotional or management constraint is to make clear that the purpose of the discussion is to analyze and clarify the constraint. Emphasize that a decision has not been made and won't be until all concerned are clear about the issues involved. As with the other procedures suggested for career change, this doesn't always work. It is, however, a means of increasing the probabilities for clear communication and for obtaining a mutual understanding of the purpose of the conversation. Emotional and management constraints in and of themselves may be threatening. To add to the situation, confusion regarding the purpose one has in discussing the issue invites needless problems.

Finally, let us reiterate that some constraint statements are not expressions of underlying values but they may be related to values or desires. For example, as we indicated, the statement, "I want to become a military officer, but I cannot because I'm over the maximum age limit of thirty for OCS" made by a person forty years old is in fact a constraint. One could ask, however, why do you want to be a military officer in the first place? What value or desire is behind your career aspiration? If the answer is "I like order, enjoy changing assignments, and want to travel," then the person's age becomes less of a constraint. True, it rules out one alternative for satisfying the aspiration, but not all others. One can identify or construct many careers which would meet the three values mentioned.

Identifying the underlying values and assumptions of constraint statements and translating them into a description of contingent conditions is not a magic formula for eliminating constraints. What identifying underlying values can do is to help us avoid thinking in terms of absolutes and set the stage for identifying alternative means of achieving changes which we desire.

As with most human concerns, career change constraints frequently involve vague language and unclear values. Almost everything with which we have contact or concern is in part a function of the language we use. When our language is vague, our understanding of whatever the language depicts is also often unclear or confused. Constraints are better understood if we can describe them clearly.

chapter 6

To Do
or
Not to Do

We want to concentrate on the decision-making process in this chapter. We will combine some of the ideas previously discussed with those yet to be introduced under the general rubric of decision-making skills. Literally speaking, a decision is made in an instant, and in that sense actual decisions are but one tiny part of what we label the decision-making process. The process begins either as an urge within ourself or as a demand to or interest in responding to some outside event or circumstance. A variety of activities, both physical and mental, follow and eventually a decision is made (or not made). The decision is made in that instant when we change from a condition of not knowing whether we will do something to one of intending to do it (or not to do it). Reversals may follow. That is, we may decide to change our decision. Eventually, if the decision is made to do "something," we may do it. Implementation represents the final part of the process for a given decision.

Many people go through life without implementing important (to them) decisions. There is a philosophical position from which it can be argued that a decision not implemented is not a decision. Intentions are fine, goes the argument, but action is the important thing. Until action can be observed, no one—including the "decider"—has proof that a decision was made.

Even though that may provide a basis for an interesting philosophical discussion, it doesn't help us here. We are willing to grant that a decision has been made when the condition changes from "I'm uncertain whether I will do something," to "I intend to do it (or not do it)." Moving from the first to the second condition is often difficult enough in itself. Thus, we will treat making decisions and implementing decisions separately.

In this chapter our focus is on whatever it is that happens between the "urge or demand to change," noted earlier, and the instant when we change from a condition of uncertainty to a condition of certainty.

Decisions, regarding careers and other situations, can be difficult, frustrating, and even upsetting. Why? What accounts for decisions often being difficult tasks? One explanation is that decisions, by definition, entail predictions and predictions involve uncertainty. Many people are uncomfortable with uncertainty. A decision implies the prediction, "If I do A, then B will occur." For example, "If I marry Jane, then I will be happier than if I don't marry Jane." "If I go to college, then I will live a better life than if I don't go to college." "If I accept the position with Xerox, then I will have more opportunity for advancement than if I accept the position with Home Town Enterprises."

If we knew what we wanted, and if we were certain that A would lead to B, then the decision of whether to do A would not be difficult. Often, however, we are not sure what we want and, especially regarding career decisions, we usually are uncertain that A will lead to B. We may think that A will lead to B, but we're not sure. That's what we mean by prediction.

There are two kinds of information upon which we base career decisions. The first is information regarding the pre-decision situation, and the second is our evaluation of possible outcomes of the decisions. Prior to a career decision we may have factual information, the advice of others, our own experience, expert judgments, and wishful thinking. To some combination of these we add our feelings about the possible outcome of the decision. How strong is our desire for B? What would be lost if we decided to do (invest in) A but B failed to occur? In other words, what are we risking if we decide to do A? The difficulty of a decision, then, is a function of:

- The clarity of our objectives.
- The quality of our predictive information. (How certain are we that doing A will lead to B?)
- The importance of the outcome.
- The risk involved (what we can lose).

For example, let's suppose we are trying to decide whether to spend the afternoon playing golf or going to a movie.

1. Clarity of our objective
   - we want to have a pleasant afternoon and don't especially care how

2. Predictive information
   - the weather report calls for rain (70 percent chance)
   - a movie reviewer with whom we usually agree gives the film a favorable rating

3. The importance of the outcome
   - not serious, although it is our only free afternoon this week

4. The risk
   - about $2.00 to $3.00 either way

Ha! An easy decision! The movie wins hands down.

Now consider this one. We are trying to decide whether to purchase a vacation cabin as a means of strengthening family relationships and getting the children out of the city on weekends.

1. Clarity of objectives
   - we know that we want to help the children avoid serious trouble

and to have some positive experiences, but cannot be much more specific

2. Predictive information

- we know four families who purchased vacation places; two appeared to enjoy theirs, the children in the third refused to go, and the parents in the fourth got a divorce
- the salesman says its an ideal place
- the kids are already showing signs of undesirable behavior

3. The importance of the outcome

- the kids are running with a bad crowd and may get into serious trouble unless some new activity is initiated to change their associations, or so we think

4. The risk

- it is more than we can easily afford; we'll have to borrow $5,000 for a down payment and repairs in addition to making monthly payments; might get it back, but it would take time; property isn't moving well.

Obviously, this is a difficult decision for several reasons. Our objectives are not clear; the predictive information is weak; the outcome appears important; and a significant amount of money would be risked. There is, in other words, much uncertainty.

As suggested earlier, clarifying and improving the four kinds of information (objectives, predictive information, values, and risks) can often decrease the uncertainty of career decisions. However, it is important to remember that most career change decisions which are significant will also involve some uncertainty because, after all, they entail predictions.

DECISION-MAKING STYLES

We hesitate for any purpose to divide the world into kinds of people. Having hesitated, we want to describe five kinds of decision-making styles, recognizing that a person who would fit any one perfectly probably doesn't exist. To the extent that one style or another does describe how we typically go about making decisions, the classification may serve to clarify past decision-making behavior.

Intuitive Style

Intuitive decision makers are a joy to observe. They examine one aspect of a situation and then another, seeming to enjoy the whole process while many of the rest of us dutifully translate complaints to objectives, clarify constraints, and consider alternate means of achieving our goals. The intuitive decision maker's secret is that he knows that all of the motions he goes through prior to the instant of decision are totally unrelated to what he will do during the instant of decision. He's looking for one thing and one thing only. The intuitive decision maker is waiting until a particular choice "feels right," and when it does, he is relatively confident that he has made the "right" decision. The decision is made quickly and with a flourish and ease that many of us resent. Many intuitive decision makers frequently seem pleased with their lot in life. They enjoy living. Some other intuitive decision makers appear to be continuously in difficulty, bailing themselves out of one ineffective decision after another. The chief reason for the difference, one might speculate, is what else the intuitive decision makers have going for themselves. Personal and material resources plus a creative imagination, for example, can go a long way toward achieving the objective of a career change decision which without them would be disastrous. That is, some intuitive decision makers seem to have sufficient imagination, creativity, and adaptive ability and resources that making a "right" decision is much less important than what they do following the decision.

Appeal-to-Authority Style

If the intuitive decision maker is a joy to observe, the appeal-to-authority decision maker presents a painful display of frustration. This person isn't any more concerned with objectives and constraints than the intuitive decision maker, and he is also in search of a particular solution to his problem. He is searching for advice from someone who "knows the right decision" to make. This wouldn't be a bad decision-making style, except for two additional characteristics of the appeal-to-authority decision maker. One of these is that after having obtained advice, he invariably has doubts regarding its quality. He manifests this doubt in a variety of ways. Sometimes he says to himself, "Hey! I don't think this guy knows any more about the situation than I do." Other times he expresses his doubt by asking, "Now really, I mean really, do you think this is the right thing to do? I really want your advice."

The second characteristic which keeps the appeal-to-authority decision maker in a state of indecision is his expectation that there is always one more person whose advice will be better than any he has obtained so far. His search for advice never ends.

Fatalistic Style

One of the most admirable decision-making styles is the fatalist. The fatalistic decision maker has real courage. He operates on the basis that it doesn't make a damn bit of difference what he does anyhow, so let it happen. His slogan is, "Screw It." **Fatalistic decision makers avoid a great deal of frustration and wear and tear on their nervous system because they actually make few decisions.** They aren't very concerned about those they do make, suspecting all along that even in these instances some mistake has been made and eventually it will be obvious that events were predetermined.

Impulsive Style

The impulsive decision maker may seem at first glance to be similar to the intuitive type. But that's not true. The intuitive types think about their decisions and examine all kinds of alternatives in their search for what "feels right." Impulsive decision makers, in contrast, aren't searching for anything. Their efforts are devoted entirely to avoiding any consideration of a decision until it has to be made. Impulsive decision makers often have many nervous mannerisms. For example, they hum a lot, start but never finish many books, tap their feet even when there isn't any music, and spend much time thinking about insignificant events. In effect, they are stalling and at the same time preparing for the next decision which will confront them. When the inescapable moment finally arrives, their mind is free of any preconsiderations and they are able to decide upon the basis of whatever has the most appeal at the time. When the decision is made, the impulsive decision maker returns instantly to toe-tapping and thinking about insignificant events, thus stalling and waiting for the next moment of decision.

Rational Style

Finally, we come to rational decision makers. **Rational decision makers make such effective and efficient decisions that they make some people sick.** Rational decision makers use the concepts and skills described in these pages. They take them seriously. They plan a great deal more than other kinds of decision makers. Their careers are characterized by knowing what they will probably be doing a day, week, month, or year from now. Rational decision makers put a lot of faith in the cause-effect notion. They think that things just don't happen, but rather that one thing(s) causes another, and that one can influence what happens in the future by behaving purposefully in the present. Rational decision makers put a lot of stock in clarifying career objectives and obtaining relevant information before making a decision. Also, they are able to accept uncertainty as a fact of life. As suggested, they can be a disgusting bunch.

These verbal caricatures of five kinds of decision makers at least illustrate that there is no single way to make career change decisions. While the writers' biases are obvious, we nevertheless support the contention that for some individuals a rational decision-making style would be inappropriate—or at least not very useful. The world has many floaters and drifters and wait-and-seers, and probably always will. Nevertheless, to the extent that you desire to use a rational decision-making style, the following may be helpful.

RATIONAL DECISION-MAKING

A simple example of a rational decision-making process applied to a personal issue is provided by the procedure followed by many life insurance salespersons. It may serve as a point of reference for many readers. In this situation the decision maker (customer) usually has a simple objective, namely, to provide adequate financial resources for her family should he or she die prior to each family member reaching an age at which she could be responsible for her own well-being. The salesperson first asks you to clarify your objective—to define what is meant by "adequate financial resources." The definition is neat and clean—so many dollars per year, decreasing each year according to the expected needs of dependents. The salesperson then gathers information about your existing financial resources such as retirement income, Social Security, savings, and investments. He then sends all of this information regarding objectives and resources to a computer for analysis. He offers you three alternatives. Plan A provides maximum protection, completely achieving your goal. Plan B adequately meets your objectives if your spouse is gainfully employed. Plan C is a cheapie thrown in to salvage something out of his sales effort even if you don't care enough about your family to provide them with adequate protection. The decision to be made is clear. You know both the cost and benefits of each plan. Take your choice. Uncertainty exists, but uncertainty accompanies all significant decisions.

A Decision-Making Procedure—Nine Steps and a Worksheet

The procedure used to make the decision just illustrated involved several specific steps. In our illustration some steps were more apparent than others. It is probably obvious that some steps overlap others. Nevertheless, for purposes of learning a rational decision-making procedure, it is useful to identify each step separately, and initially, at least, to practice each by itself.

Remember that the procedure is concerned with deciding upon an alternative for pursuing a career change goal, not with developing a plan for doing the alternative selected. The latter is a matter of implementing decisions and is the concern of the next chapter.

Try to avoid confusing a goal with an alternative means of pursuing it. For example, "obtaining a college degree," "getting a job," and "securing a divorce" are usually not goals. Sometimes they are, but usually each represents only one means of achieving a basic goal. Obtaining a college degree, for example, is usually one means of gaining status or preparing for a job or becoming better informed. There are alternative means of achieving each of these three goals. The same idea applies to the other two examples. "Getting a job" is one alternative means for achieving goals such as acquiring money or engaging in a worthwhile activity. And "securing a divorce" is only one means of reaching the goal of resolving marital unhappiness. This idea is not always easy to grasp. It is not unusual, in other words, to confuse a goal with one means of pursuing it. When we do, of course, we become preoccupied with that alternative and tend to ignore others, some of which may be much more suitable to our actual goal. Keep this idea in mind as you use the nine-step decision-making procedure.

The nine steps of the procedure are described below, followed by an illustration. Referring to the "Career Decision Worksheet" (Table 21) as you read the following can help clarify the procedure.

1. *State Your Goal.* Translate complaints into goals. Describe "how you would like things to be." Note examples. Identify both existing negative conditions and missing desired conditions. Then record a clear and specific statement of your goal in space 1 on Table 21. If you have identified several goals or problems, select the one that you want to work on first.

2. *Identify Alternatives.* List every possible alternative means of achieving the goal you can think of in space 2. If you can't think of any, ask others for suggestions and seek out information whenever possible (see Chapter 8). Regardless of how impractical or foolish some may appear, list them anyway. Hold off on value judgments.

3. *Clean Up Alternatives.* Now review your list of alternatives. Combine those which appear redundant, and eliminate any which are so much in conflict with your values that you can't accept them. Use the constraints analysis procedure in Chapter 5 to clarify underlying values.

4. *Predict Needed Resources.* In space 3 note the resources needed to implement each alternative. Don't overlook personal resources such as persistence, courage, support from others, and self-confidence. This

often requires obtaining information regarding some or all of the alternatives.

5. *Be Realistic.* Eliminate alternatives for which resources are clearly unavailable or which you believe to be too difficult to acquire. (Again, use the constraints analysis procedure in Chapter 5 to clarify your judgments.)

6. *Identify Risks.* In space 4 note the risks and undesirable aspects entailed in each remaining alternative. Risks refer to what you might lose by pursuing each alternative. Include things such as self-esteem and relationships as well as material items. "Undesirable aspects" include such considerations as being inconvenienced or dealing with unpleasant circumstances.

7. *Evaluate Risks.* Now use space 5 to rate each remaining alternative according to your willingness to accept the risk or experience the undesirable aspects involved. Use the following scale:

1 = acceptable
2 = mostly acceptable—some reservations
3 = mostly unacceptable—very uncomfortable with it
4 = totally unacceptable

Rule out all alternatives rated 4.

8. *Select.* Now, if you want to make a decision with minimum risk, select the alternative which has the most acceptable risk level and for which resources can be obtained. (If two or more alternatives have similar ratings, go to step 9.)

9. *Introduce Your Values.* If low risk is not your most important consideration, then do an alternatives preference ranking. To do this, first record the basis of your preference in space 6. (Preference can range from "impact on others" to "it feels good.") Then use space 7 to rank the alternatives according to your preference and without regard to the level of risk involved. Your first preference will be ranked Number 1, your second Number 2, and so on. Now choose the alternative which has the highest preference ranking *and* an acceptable risk rating.

The decision-making procedures can be learned with a little practice. Before using the nine steps, it should be helpful to study the following illustration.

TABLE 21. Career Decision Worksheet

1. OBJECTIVE

2. ALTERNATIVES	3. RESOURCES NEEDED			
	SKILLS	MONEY	PERSONAL	OTHER

6. PREFERENCE CRITERIA

4. RISKS AND UNDESIRABLE ASPECTS	5. RISK RATING	7. PREFER-ENCE RANKING

Ann is married and has three children. She married the same month she graduated from high school ten years ago. The first baby came ten months after that, and the third baby arrived before her fourth wedding anniversary. Bob, her husband, began his junior year in college shortly after they were married. The initial two years were difficult, but they did survive by borrowing from their parents, obtaining a loan, and Bob working part-time. He completed his B.A. in Business Administration and a satisfying life-style was in sight. During the intervening years, Bob has worked for a large retail department store where he is currently an assistant manager in charge of business operations. He is often preoccupied with job concerns. Their debts to their parents and the loan have been paid off, and two years ago they began purchasing a comfortable three-bedroom home.

Doesn't sound so bad, does it? Well, Ann's life has changed quite a bit in the last few months. Their youngest child is now in school, and Ann spends a great portion of each day alone. Her enthusiasm about decorating the house and gardening has dwindled. Her relationship with Bob has been deteriorating for several years and has become particularly strained in the last few months—to the point that they are discussing divorce as a solution. Their discussions have not led to a productive solution.

Ann realizes that other than her attempts to discuss the marriage relationship with her husband, she has done nothing to deal with her career dissatisfactions. Now determined to obtain greater satisfaction, she has begun to analyze her situation as a basis for making career change decisions. In the following pages we have noted some of her thinking as she has used the decision-making procedure and completed her Career Decision Worksheet (Table 22).

State Your Goal

Ann began by noting several goals such as getting a job and joining volunteer groups. Then she realized that these weren't goals, but alternative means for obtaining "something else." After considerable thought she listed the following goals:

- To improve the marriage relationship or to resolve it in some way to diminish the unhappiness it caused.
- To develop new sources of career satisfaction which would provide a sense of contribution and worth.

After further thought, she assigned top priority to the first goal and entered it on her Career Decision Worksheet. The second goal, while important, would be put aside until she made some progress on the first.

Identify Alternatives

Ann began by listing alternate ways to reach her goal. The first list contained these items:

- Go to a marriage counselor with Bob.
- Go to our minister with Bob.
- Talk to other married friends about how they relate to each other.
- Try a trial separation.
- File for a divorce.

After talking with a friend, Ann added these alternatives:

- Jointly read and try the ideas/techniques described in such books as *Marriage Happiness* and *The Mirages of Marriage*.
- Join a couples group sponsored by the YMCA.
- Devise an approach on their own for establishing effective ways to relate.

Ann thought this list probably was not exhaustive, but it seemed to contain a fair number of alternatives to consider.

Clean Up Alternatives

Ann then reviewed her list for the purpose of identifying redundancies and clearly unacceptable alternatives. She rejected the last alternative on the list because it represented essentially the procedure they had been following. She also rejected the alternative of a trial separation because this seemed to be little more than postponing dealing with the problem. She entered the remaining alternatives on her worksheet as shown.

Predict Needed Resources

The next step was to determine what kind of resources would be needed for each remaining alternative. This took much time and effort on her part, and she found that it was necessary to imagine living each of the alternatives before she could identify all the resources that would be needed. The most difficult resources to pinpoint were the personal/emotion resources that would be required if each alternative became a reality. To do this she imagined the kind of interactions and negotiations that might occur with each alternative and, then, based on past experience, she predicted how she might react in the situations. On that basis she predicted the emotional resources which would be needed. The list that she developed is shown on page 108.

TABLE 22. Ann's Career Decision Worksheet

1. OBJECTIVE	To improve marriage relationship or resolve it in some way to diminish unhappiness it causes

2. ALTER-NATIVES	3. RESOURCES NEEDED			
	SKILLS	MONEY	PERSONAL	OTHER
Marriage counselor	Ability to select competent counselor Ability to describe why I think this would be an effective alternative to Bob	$25 an hour	Courage to overcome initial fear of talking to "outsider"	Bob's cooperation
Minister	Ability to describe why I think this would be an effective alternative to Bob	None	Courage to overcome being embarrassed to describe personal problems to minister	Bob's cooperation
Talk to friends	Ability to describe why I think this would be an effective alternative to Bob Ability to describe to friends how and what we want to talk about	None	Courage to overcome embarrassment of describing personal problems to friends	Bob's cooperation
Divorce	Ability to describe to Bob why I think this would be an effective alternative Ability to make new life-style for self—social, work skills Ability to be single parent	Lawyer's fees Funds for separate household for Bob Child support and alimony	Courage and skill to deal with loneliness Reactions of friends and family	
Read books: Use techniques	Ability to describe why I think this would be an effective alternative to Bob Ability to jointly discuss and implement ideas presented	Minimal	Self-confidence to engage in intellectual discussion with Bob	Bob's cooperation
Couples group	Ability to describe why I think this would be an effective alternative to Bob Ability to discuss concerns in group	$30 for 6-week series	Courage to describe personal problems to strangers	Bob's cooperation

| 6. PREFERENCE CRITERIA | 1. Quality of help |
| | 2. Non-involvement of other people |

4. RISKS AND UNDESIRABLE ASPECTS	5. RISK RATING	7. PREFER-ENCE RANKING
Might make situation worse by opening areas previously unopened Might argue over spending $25 an hour	2	1
I know minister much better than Bob Might make situation worse by opening areas previously unopened Might strain current friendly relationship with minister Minister might not have training in marriage counseling	3	3
Might endanger our current friendly relationships with couples Might make our relationship worse by opening areas previously unopened Might start disagreements between the other couples involved	3	5
Might make situation worse by opening areas previously unopened Might cause arguments of "You're not using the idea/technique right"	2	2
Might make situation worse by opening areas previously unopened Might get unqualified or ineffective group leader	3	4

Be Realistic

The next task was to eliminate alternatives for which there were inadequate resources or for which the resources were too difficult to obtain. After reviewing the list, Ann decided that there was really only one alternative—divorce—for which the resources were not available. Ann felt that at the present time she did not have the necessary occupational skills, financial resources, or self-confidence to start a new life-style as a single parent. Thus, she eliminated this alternative.

Identify Risks

In the next decision-making phase Ann enumerated the risks and undesirable aspects in each alternative. Again she found that she had to mentally estimate what would be involved. Her list of risks and undesirable aspects is on page 109.

Evaluate Risks

Ann rated the risks for each of the remaining alternatives, using the following four-point scale. As shown on the chart, Ann had no 4 ratings.

1 = acceptable
2 = mainly acceptable—some reservations
3 = mostly unacceptable—very uncomfortable with it
4 = totally unacceptable

Select

Ann still had five alternatives for which she could probably obtain the resources and which had acceptable risks. If she had been seeking a low-risk decision, then at this point she would have rejected the three alternatives with risk ratings of 3, and decided between the first and fourth alternatives. However, because she was not primarily interested in a low-risk decision, she was willing to consider all of the five remaining alternatives.

Introduce Your Values

She ranked the five remaining alternatives in terms of her preference. The criteria she used were: (a) quality of assistance and (b) noninvolvement of friends and people other than Bob and herself. Her ranking is noted in space 6 on the Career Decision Worksheet. As shown, she ranked seeing a marriage counselor as the preferred alternative.

If the decision-making procedure is appealing, we suggest that you try it with an actual or imaginary decision. If the procedure doesn't lead to a satisfactory decision, reviewing your worksheet may clarify something you have overlooked or omitted from your decision-making effort. Reviewing your worksheet in regard to values clarification, the possibility of multiple decisions, the investment required, and the uncertainty involved may be especially helpful. The following paragraphs clarify each of these four sources of decision-making difficulty.

Are you clear about the values underlying the decision? A careful review of spaces 4 and 6 on the worksheet may help identify values which are important but not yet considered. Have you listed all of the things (material goods, relationships, personal characteristics) which might be lost or damaged? Have you noted all of the undesirable aspects of each alternative? **In other words, are you being honest with yourself?** That may not be an easy guideline to follow because in doing so all kinds of frustrating and painful issues that would be unpleasant to deal with may be raised. Nevertheless, refusing to admit serious sources of career dissatisfaction seriously inhibits making significant career changes. For example, career counselors frequently encounter clients who have spent a good number of years making one job change after another in search of greater career satisfaction. Some, aided by the counselor's objectivity and sensitive questioning, are able to acknowledge (perhaps for the first time even to themselves) that the basic source of their career dissatisfaction is not the job component but rather problems regarding marriage or family relationships; resentment regarding accomplishment of relatives or friends; or some other concern. If such sources of dissatisfaction exist but are ignored and job change receives all the attention, we can expect to feel ambivalent about career change alternatives, and thus find career change decisions especially difficult to make.

Sometimes decisions are unnecessarily difficult because the decision we are trying to make is in fact a combination of several decisions. Such general decisions are usually more difficult to make than specific decisions. We can struggle unsuccessfully with a general decision when in fact we could deal separately with the several specific decisions involved. Consider the following example.

John was nearing completion of a twenty-year career in the military. He knew that he had to decide "what to do after retirement," but was no closer to making that decision now than he was six months ago. His frustration was mounting. To make a long story short, a counselor assisted John in substituting a series of more specific decisions for the larger one on which he was making no progress. The list of more specific decisions John generated included the desire to decide:

- Where he wanted to live
- How much money he wanted
- What personal goals were most important
- How much time to devote to an occupation
- What would be the best situation for his family.

John was able to make tentative decisions regarding each specific issue with relative ease. He then engaged in a process of comparing and trading one against the other until he was able to "decide what to do after retirement."

If the decision on which you have been working is actually a multiple decision, try to state and work on each specific issue separately.

There are times when the probable outcomes of a decision don't appear to justify the investment of resources required to implement it. It may be, in other words, that living with present conditions may be more attractive than expending the effort to change. Such a conclusion may be difficult to accept, especially if you hold the belief that there is some "perfect" solution to all career change problems. If you can accept, on the other hand, that there are probably few absolutely perfect solutions, then it may be easier to conclude that your present situation, even with its undesirable conditions, is more desirable (or less undesirable) than any of your alternatives.

Finally, we return to the matter of uncertainty. Is your inability to reach an acceptable decision due to your unwillingness to accept the uncertainty of the alternatives leading to your desired outcome? An unwillingness to accept uncertainty regarding the outcomes of decisions can immobilize us in making career changes. The issue is treated in Chapter 7 which describes several procedures for implementing career decisions.

It should be clear by now, if not before, that making rational career decisions can be complex; but then so is the concern of such decisions, namely life itself. The procedures described in this chapter won't make decisions for you. No procedure can do that. They can, however, provide a means for increasing your effectiveness in dealing with complex career decisions.

chapter 7

Making a Difference:

Implementing Career Decisions

The real payoff of a decision comes when you put it into action. But that is not always as easy as it may sound. Why are career change decisions often difficult to implement, especially if they have been made carefully and rationally? There are many explanations, but we believe that the following accurately summarize the most common obstacles.

- We don't know where to begin.
- There seem to be so many things to do at once that confusion soon reigns and makes us ineffective.
- The length of time between when we begin our effort and when we finally achieve our goals is so great that we become discouraged and lose interest.
- We lack means for dealing with unfamiliar situations.

These are the kinds of implementation problems with which we will be concerned in this chapter. We will discuss and illustrate methods for *getting started, planning, maintaining motivation,* and *dealing with unfamiliar situations.*

GETTING STARTED

Finding an appropriate starting place and taking action is the first step in implementing a career decision. One effective procedure is to do a quick overview of the tasks and considerations which will be involved in your implementation effort. The Implementation Overview (Table 23) was designed to help you with this task. To begin, enter today's date. Next note the career decision you have made. What have you decided to do? You may want to record the larger goal of your decision, or perhaps only its first phase. For example, while your larger decision may be to complete a one-year training course, implementation may be more effective if you concentrate on completing the first term of study. Whether you decide to consider the total decision or some smaller aspect of it, set a target date. Then, without regard to any time sequence, note your responses to the six categories on the form. When you have completed this exercise, you have begun implementing your decision. If the decision is a relatively simple one, completing the Implementation Overview may be all that is needed.

In the case of more complex decisions, you may want to translate the notes made on your Overview into a more specific implementation plan as described below.

TABLE 23. Implementation Overview

Today's Date	Career Decision	Target Date

Information to be obtained	Money and personal resources required
Skills and abilities required	Time commitments
Arrangements to be made	Other decisions to be made

PLANNING

A critical aspect of planning is that of committing your intended actions to paper. Generally speaking, a written plan is more effective than one unwritten. Writing tends to clarify, add specificity, and help identify gaps or missing parts. One way to be precise is to note the action to be taken at each step in the plan. In other words, use verbs. Also, try to break each part of your plan into smaller parts. For example, if one of your steps is "gather information about employers," a more precise description of what is involved might read:

- *List* employers of interest
- *Write* for company brochures
- *Read* professional journals for articles about companies of interest
- *Request* interviews with representatives of companies
- *Talk* to an employee of each company for more information

To facilitate planning, it is useful to estimate the amount of time for accomplishing each step in the plan. For example, consider a person who made the decision to obtain a management trainee position. His implementation plan might look at follows:

IMPLEMENTATION PLAN

Action to be taken:

Complete placement credential file.. estimated time: 2 weeks

Complete a resumé................ estimated time: 2 weeks

Sharpen interview skills............ estimated time: 1 week

Develop list of potential employers.. estimated time: 2 weeks

Research these employers.......... estimated time: 2 weeks

Do job interviews................ estimated time: 6 weeks

Some career changes may be too difficult to plan using only simple lists. In such instances, when several things must be done simultaneously, the use of a time line can be helpful. A time line provides for a two-dimensional display of the activities to be done. The visual display of the overlapping activities helps many people develop a clearer understanding of the various aspects of their plan. The following example illustrates the use of a time line, as displayed on page 118.

Helen is the mother of two children and has been divorced for nearly a year. She had given a good deal of thought to the problems of restructuring her life and after examining various possibilities and alternatives decided to obtain a position in the general field of human resources, such as a counselor or case worker. She learned that an additional year of education would be necessary in order to compete successfully for a position. She would need to complete several tasks over the next twelve months. She developed the following plan, using the time line concept. Her general plan was supported by a list of more specific tasks, as illustrated in Table 24. For example, she noted that registering with the college placement office would involve preparing a resumé, obtaining several strong letters of reference, and establishing a good relationship with a member of the placement office staff to help assure that she was more than a number.

A written plan is a way of "getting it all together." Having a plan doesn't guarantee that the decision to make a career change will be implemented, but it does clarify what must be done.

TABLE 24. Helen's Implementation Plan

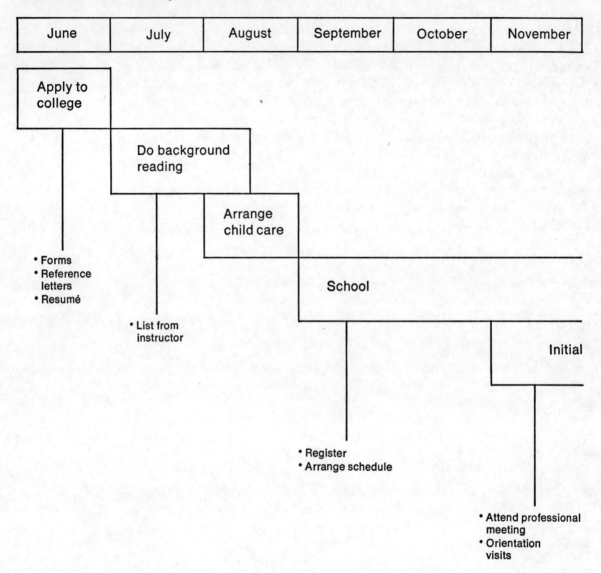

June	July	August	September	October	November

Apply to college

Do background reading

Arrange child care

- Forms
- Reference letters
- Resumé

- List from instructor

School

- Register
- Arrange schedule

Initial

- Attend professional meeting
- Orientation visits

December	January	February	March	April	May

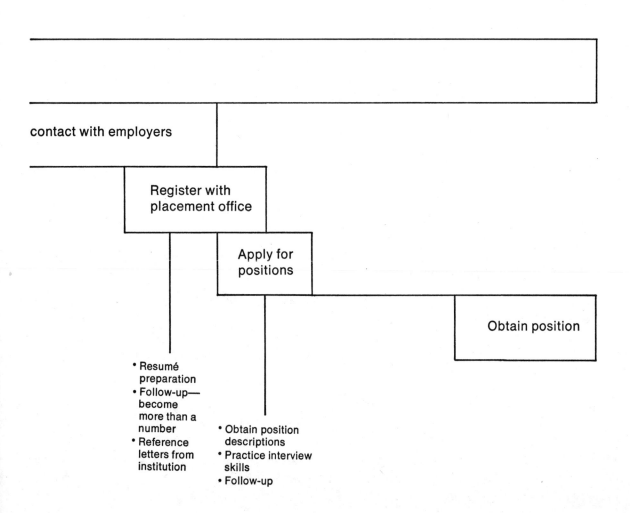

contact with employers

Register with
placement office

Apply for
positions

Obtain position

- Resumé
  preparation
- Follow-up—
  become
  more than a
  number
- Reference
  letters from
  institution

- Obtain position
  descriptions
- Practice interview
  skills
- Follow-up

MAINTAINING MOTIVATION

Many tasks involved in implementing career decisions have no immediate reward or payoff. For example, writing a resumé, researching employers, and attending a job interview workshop may seem only vaguely related to obtaining a specific position. Because of the lack of immediate rewards, many people cannot maintain adequate motivation to complete the steps in their implementation plan. When this happens it is often helpful to establish some intermediate rewards as a means of maintaining motivation. In other words, you can develop a self-reward system when "natural" rewards are missing.

The concept of self-reward involves choosing a pleasant experience and using it to reward yourself after you have completed a desired activity. For example, you might reward yourself for completing a resumé by taking a bike ride, visiting friends, or going out to dinner. Planning such rewards can help you stay with your plan until it has been completed. There are three general principles for developing a reward system.

- The reward should be consistent. Haphazard rewarding, in which the desired activity is sometimes rewarded and sometimes not, is less effective than providing a reward each time the activity is performed.
- The reward should be provided as soon after completing the activity as possible. The point is to associate the reward (satisfying experience) with doing the desired activity.
- The reward should be clearly linked to the activity. Being specific about both the activity and the reward helps clarify the linkage.

Obviously the interim reward should be something which you value as pleasant or satisfying and should be readily accessible. The following examples illustrate the use of interim reward.

A woman enrolled in several classes in order to prepare herself for a job. Her courses required about an hour of reading each day. The reading, however, was not particularly interesting and she often put it off. This had a negative effect on her course work. Consequently, she established the following interim reward system.

Desired Activity	*Reward*
Read 60 minutes (11:00 A.M.–12 M. each day)	View the noon news on TV

Viewing the news program was an enjoyable activity, and she made doing this activity contingent upon doing the reading.

A retired couple decided to engage in foreign travel. Their goal was two trips per year. This could be accomplished only by reducing their current monthly expenditures, which in turn required that they cooperatively prepare a budget at the beginning of each month. This was a task neither enjoyed doing. Thus they established the following interim reward system.

Desired Activity	Reward
Prepare monthly budget on first of the month	Trip to library to borrow travel books
Review budget and expenditures on the 15th	Attend local travel film or slide presentation

Another type of reward is illustrated by a person who decided to begin a search for a new job. **Job searches involve a variety of tasks, some of which can be tedious and unpleasant.** From past experience this person suspected that he would procrastinate beginning the job search tasks. Therefore, the individual listed the tasks that were involved and assigned dollar values to each, as indicated below.

Activity	Value
Prepare resumé	$5
Visit Placement Office	$5
Write letter to employer	$2
Obtain reference	$5
Monitor ads in newspapers and journals	$2
Complete job interview	$5

He then deposited $75, which he would normally spend for nonessential items, into a savings account and established a rule that each time a task was done he could reward himself by withdrawing the designated amount from his savings.

The usefulness of rewards is not limited to changes in the job and vocation aspects of career. New leisure time activities sometimes are not immediately rewarding and may be abandoned before you develop sufficient skill or involvement for the activity to be rewarding. One person, for example, decided to enroll in a leather craft class, but was so discouraged after the first class that she considered dropping the activity. Her instructor suggested that she persist for several sessions and give herself a chance to become more involved. He also suggested that after attending each class she reward herself by purchasing an inexpensive, illustrated paperback book on leather working.

The woman followed his suggestion, and by the fourth week she was looking forward to attending class. The simple reward helped her sustain her interest until she gained sufficient skills to make leather working satisfying.

So far we have illustrated relatively simple uses of rewards. The following example illustrates the use of interim rewards in a more complex career change situation.

A family of five decided to make a major career change—moving from the city to a rural area. A dramatic change in life-style would be involved for all members of the family. While the ultimate expectations were high, they predicted that many aspects of the change would not be rewarding, and that others would be unpleasant. They outlined the many tasks involved and developed a schedule for completing them. Whenever possible they assigned specific responsibility for each task to a family member. The reward for completing these tasks was a restaurant dinner and conversation about their anticipated change at the end of each week. The conversation was part fact and part fantasy, but more important it was an enjoyable experience. However, the dinner outing was made only after each family member had performed his tasks for the week.

Sometimes an interim reward system can be made more effective by using another person to provide the reward. One can make either an oral or written contract with an associate who will give you a specified reward when the desired activity is performed. In addition to reducing the chances of cheating, the use of a contract also involves another person in the career change plan. This in itself can be rewarding. An obvious risk in contracting, however, is resenting or being angry at the person designated for withholding the reward when the desired activity is not completed. It is wise, therefore, to examine the nature of your underlying relationship with another person before asking him to contract with you.

DEALING WITH UNFAMILIAR SITUATIONS

So far in this chapter we have discussed procedures for getting started, planning, and maintaining motivation to continue an implementation plan. Even when these procedures have been used, we can still encounter obstacles standing in the way of implementing our decisions. Many of these barriers consist, in one way or another, of our needing to deal with unfamiliar situations. Consequently, the remainder of this chapter will be devoted to a discussion of several skills which we have found useful in assisting people to deal with unfamiliar situations encountered in making career changes. The skills consist of *previewing, role playing, modeling,* and *debriefing.*

Previewing

Previewing is closely related to planning, but more immediate. Planning outlines a relatively long-range view of implementing career change. Previewing, in comparison, refers to thinking through the behavior and circumstances involved in the specific activity in which you are about to engage. The purpose of previewing is to sharpen your awareness of what will be required in the situation, determine how these requirements might be met, and clarify what you expect to achieve. Previewing can be especially helpful when you are particularly anxious about the anticipated situation. Job interviews, the first day on the job, a discussion concerning a family problem, or the first day in class are examples of the kinds of situations in which previewing can be helpful. Previewing obviously includes making predictions about what will be involved in a given situation; and as is the nature of predictions, they may be inaccurate. That is not particularly important because the point of previewing is to focus on one's self—not to imagine all that might go wrong. One can usually predict accurately some parts of the forthcoming situation. Previewing simply provides a little simulated experience in dealing with it.

Previewing is illustrated by an employment interview training program for college women. The women in the program were completing their last year of college and anticipated being interviewed by possible employers. They were provided a list of questions which they might be asked, and were instructed to think through the response that they would make. The list included questions such as "What are your plans for marriage?" "How do you feel about women's liberation?" and "How would you react to having to work irregular hours?" The women were able to organize their thoughts about these and other questions and to formulate tentative answers. As a result they had a better basis for responding to potential interviewer questions.

Another student in a similar program was a severe stutterer. He was encouraged to preview an employment interview with particular attention to dealing with the recruiters' potential reaction (overt or covert) to his speech problem. This particular student, after previewing the anticipated situation, decided to introduce the subject himself early in the interview, thus demonstrating to the recruiter that while he had a problem, he was also willing to acknowledge it and had a means of coping with it.

In another setting, a woman who had worked for several years had decided to resign her job and devote most of her energy to her family for the next several years. She anticipated that the conversation in which she informed her husband of her decision might be something more than casual. Consequently, she previewed the various questions and reactions he might have and anticipated how she could effectively respond.

Previewing, in short, can contribute to both starting and maintaining the desired behavior by providing a "simulated" experience.

Role Playing

Another procedure which can be useful in initiating a career change is role playing. You may hesitate or endlessly postpone initiating an activity about which you are uncertain. Few of us enjoy risking our self-esteem, but many times initiating new behaviors involves just that. Role playing is a means by which you can practice the new behaviors in a protected environment prior to doing them in the "real situation." Role playing is helpful in preparing for situations in which personal interaction behavior will be involved, such as employment interviews, attending social or other group functions, and discussions involving critical or otherwise sensitive issues.

To do role playing you need a description of the anticipated situation and the cooperation of another person. The general procedure involves:

- Discussing the situation involved (e.g., an employment interview) and identifying the behaviors to be practiced;
- Agreeing on the roles each person is to play (e.g., "You be the applicant and I'll be the interviewer");
- Acting out the situation;
- Reviewing your performance (What did you do well; what needs improvement; how can you do better?);
- Practicing the role again, especially the behaviors needing improvement, until you are satisfied.

Identifying the behaviors to be practiced is especially important. Unless this has been done prior to role playing the situation, what takes place can be very vague and thus omit important aspects of the situation. Using the employment interview example, we might identify the following behaviors:

(1) introducing yourself; (2) describing your interests; (3) describing your qualifications; (4) asking for information about working conditions; (5) responding to unanticipated questions; (6) responding to "what would you do if" questions; (7) learning what the "next steps" will be; (8) closing the interview.

Your partner in role playing might also observe and comment on your posture, mode of dress, and physical mannerisms.

The content of role play situations will vary, but it is usually possible to predict at least some of the behaviors to be practiced. For example, consider a husband who wants to propose a significant change in his family's life-style.

By previewing the anticipated family discussion, he can probably identify reactions to his proposal. If he predicts that he may have difficulty responding to these, role playing parts of the discussion with a friend can be a helpful way to practice responses and gain confidence before initiating the discussion.

Role playing may appear "silly" to some; others may be self-conscious about trying the procedures. Given that our society conditions us not to deal directly with feelings of uncertainty and to treat feelings as something one cannot do much about, this is understandable. We would urge, however, that you try using role playing as an aid to implementing decisions before you reject it.

The Use of Models

Especially during the early years of life, the use of behavior models is a primary method of learning. Most of us learned to talk, walk, feed ourselves, and a multitude of other behaviors by observing and imitating someone else. They were our models. Using someone else as a model can be a useful procedure for implementing career decisions. It is important, however, to distinguish between "being like someone else" from "behaving similarly to another person in a given situation." The first use of modeling is often inappropriate —it is usually impossible to "take on" the personality of another person. Both they and we are too complex, and our circumstances are different. The person who attempts to "be like someone else" usually appears superficial, shallow, or pretentious.

On the other hand, you can frequently identify another person who displays a particular behavior that appears useful and related to your own objectives. In such instances you are not attempting to be the other person, but simply trying to learn a particular behavior by using him as a model.

The use of a model can be especially helpful in learning communication and personal relations skills. In addition to carefully observing the behavior which you would like to learn, it also can be helpful to ask the other person to explain how he feels about the behavior in question. For example, a student admired the ease with which a classmate engaged in classroom discussions and wished to develop this skill herself. She observed that the classmate made relatively specific comments and usually contributed new information to discussions. She asked the classmate how he was able to be so effective and apparently spontaneous. The classmate explained, much to her surprise, that his behavior wasn't all that spontaneous. He said that he made a point of reading some unassigned material related to each day's discussion and that he made a mental list of four or five contributions which he might make. Usually he found that two or three of these were pertinent to the discussion. By questioning her model, she was able to both observe and understand the basis for a desired behavior.

This example also illustrates the more basic idea that what often seems to be "natural" behaviors are in fact learned and done consciously. For example, a person who seems at ease in a tense situation may in fact be experiencing anxiety, or the person who appears self-confident may recognize the risks he is taking. Understanding this as well as seeing the behavior in question can help in learning that behavior.

Debriefing

Self-debriefing consists of a dialogue with one's self in which a number of questions are asked and answered. It involves using recent past experiences as a basis for improving performance in the future. Self-debriefing places as much emphasis on how you feel about your behavior as on its effects or results. It is "self-talk" but more than a summary or replay of what has taken place. Its primary function, rather, is an analysis of past experiences. Self-debriefing can be used to analyze a particular incident or to review behaviors occurring over a relatively long time period. Examples of both uses of self-debriefing are provided below.

Mary, a woman who had decided to obtain a part-time job as part of a career change, had just terminated an unpleasant discussion with her husband. She had completed two weeks on the job without incident. On the next Monday one of her children became ill at school. The school phoned home but was unable to reach Mary because she was at work, and so phoned her husband at his place of employment. The husband was unable to leave his job, thus the child spent several hours in the nurse's office before Mary could come for her. Mary's husband, who objected to her going to work in the first place, used the incident to support his position. He pointed out to Mary that a mother's place is in the home; he shouldn't be bothered at work by phone calls from the school; the child had been neglected; and similar incidents would undoubtedly occur in the future.

During the discussion Mary became threatened, defensive, angry, and ended up in tears. After regaining her composure she held the following self-talk debriefing session with herself.

"What was the outcome of all that?"

"I lost control and tried to defend myself by arguing that it wouldn't happen again."

"How could I have been more effective?"

"Well, I could have had some facts to counter his opinions and a plan for handling similar situations."

"What facts, for example?"

"It's the first time that the girl has ever become ill at school. She's very healthy. Given her history, it's unlikely that it will happen again."

"What plan could I propose?"

"It's not really a plan, but I could give my work phone number to the school and ask them to call me, not him. I resent that a little, but it will avoid a hassle."

"What about my reaction to his other objections to my working?"

"I should concentrate on this specific issue and not get trapped into arguing with him about his opinions. He has his, and I have mine. Neither is likely to be persuaded by the other to change."

As a result of the self-debriefing, Mary had a better basis for continuing the discussion if it became necessary. She had been able, in other words, to use her experience as an aid in learning more effective ways to implement her decision.

The following example shows how debriefing is used to review a longer time period.

Harry decided to quit community college after two semesters. He didn't enjoy his courses, felt he needed more money, and believed that further education would be of little benefit. The sooner he got to work, he told himself, the sooner he could start climbing the occupational ladder.

After about six months of working in a warehouse, Harry realized that he was more dissatisfied than when he had been in school. He did a little self-debriefing as shown in the following discourse.

"I don't like my job and see no opportunity for immediate advancement."

"Then why did I quit school?"

"I thought that I could find a job with a good future but I'm not so sure now. I also thought I needed more money, but that's not true. I just blow my salary—haven't saved anything."

"Anything else?"

"Well, I probably was a little lazy. Maybe the courses would have been more interesting if I had prepared more for them."

"What can I do about the situation?"

"I can look for a better job, or return to school and get more preparation."

"Which would be the easiest?"

"The former, probably, but I always take the easy way out. Returning to school would be more difficult, but it also makes more sense."

"How would school be any different than before?"

"It wouldn't, unless I worked harder at it."

"Can I?"

"I think so. I've learned that this kind of job isn't for me."

Debriefing can produce a renewed commitment to continuing the career change and also a clarity of purpose and increased realization that you can control your own behavior. It is also possible that a self-debriefing can be discouraging when you haven't performed as intended. Even this, however, provides a better basis for a renewed effort than ignoring and avoiding your lack of success or progress. The sooner you acknowledge that plans are not going as intended, the sooner alternatives can be developed. Thus, debriefing also provides a basis for evaluating your plan.

A final note regarding debriefing, and that is to focus on one's self—not the other people involved in a situation. The purpose of debriefing is to make your own behavior more effective. Debriefing should lead to a clearer understanding of one's purpose and values and thus improved implementation. A dialogue with one's self which is preoccupied with the faults and unfairness of others is complaining, not debriefing.

Avoiding Precipitators

A final and obvious procedure for implementing career decisions is to avoid conditions, people, events, and things which inhibit doing the desired behavior. A bar, for example, is a poor place to go for coffee for a person trying to overcome alcoholism, and, generally speaking, a person attempting to improve study habits will be more likely to do so by avoiding those to whom study habits are not important. As obvious as this notion is, some analysis and review of past events are often necessary in order to identify circumstances which precipitate undesired behaviors. It can be helpful to list such circumstances and to refer to the list from time to time as a way of anticipating situations which you may want to avoid or at least be prepared to deal with.

chapter 8

No-Change Career Changes

A self-contradictory chapter title? How can one not change, but still make a career change? The concept we want to examine in this chapter is that even when you decide that a desired major career change is not feasible at the moment there still may be things which you can do to reduce career dissatisfaction and, perhaps, even increase satisfaction. We are concerned here with situations which involve major sources of career dissatisfaction and which seem, for the time being at least, unchangeable. There are obvious examples, such as:

- An individual dissatisfied with a job, but because of his values and responsibilities is unwilling to change.

- A married couple dissatisfied with their relationship but unwilling to decide upon a divorce until their children are self-sufficient.

- A couple dissatisfied with their role as parents of teenagers but knowing that it will be several years before they will be free of such responsibilities.

- An individual dissatisfied with a training program, but unwilling to terminate it because of the anticipated benefits to be derived upon its completion.

Even in such career situations you can still initiate strategies which will make life more rewarding. Three kinds of strategies are especially useful:

- Initiating comparatively minor activities which will provide both career satisfaction in themselves, and something to which you can look forward with pleasure.

- Developing skills for coping with anticipated events and encounters which precipitate career dissatisfaction.

- Maximizing satisfaction from current satisfying activities.

It should be understood that this chapter is not simply a suggestion to "think positively." That advice is frequently obnoxious and unrealistic. While granting that perception (the way we choose to view a situation) is important, it must be acknowledged that there are career situations which are clearly dissatisfying, absurd, or miserable to almost any observer, but which are not currently changeable. To suggest to people in such situations that they think positively borders on encouraging them to become schizophrenic.

Nevertheless, doing nothing about a dissatisfying career situation frequently results in decreased mental health. Anger, frustration, depression, preoccupation with a feeling of being "trapped," and resentment are a few of the negative feelings which can develop as a result of not having something of value to substitute for a no-change decision. Such feelings can linger on for a long period of time or can change to one of general apathy or despondency. Some people give up hope of ever deriving career satisfaction; others turn to drink; and many become chronic complainers, generally negative about all aspects of their environment.

In the remainder of the chapter we will examine ways of dealing with a no-change career decision.

INITIATING NEW SATISFYING ACTIVITIES

Initiating new activities may not be as easy as it sounds. While some people seem to be forever into new and interesting pursuits, others seem perpetually bored and never able to identify new activities. Many possibly satisfying activities are so obvious that they go unnoticed. Others are essentially unknown, or at least "unthought of," to most people. In recent years serious study and research has been done on leisure activities. One study developed a classification system for leisure activities which uses the following nine categories: games, sports, nature activities, collecting, crafts, art and music, education, entertainment and cultural activities, volunteer activities, and organizational activities.[1]

It is apparent that this classification scheme fits the leisure aspect of career, and also can be extended to the vocation dimension. That is, many of the activities classified could be either leisure or vocation, depending upon the value you place on the matter.

The study referred to above produced a two-volume guide which describes hundreds of leisure activities. In addition to a description, each activity is rated according to the environmental, social-psychological, and cost factors involved. Of special interest to some readers is an indication of the extent to which various kinds of physical impairments or conditions limit doing each activity.

There is not the space here to produce an extensive list of activities. We have, however, provided a brief list for each of the nine categories, attempting to include less well-known activities.

Before looking at the list, it should be helpful to establish a frame of reference from which to perceive it. First, it is often helpful to determine whether a new activity would be more satisfying if performed alone or with

---

[1] Overs, Robert P., O'Connor, Elizabeth, and Demarco, Barbara: *Guide to Avocational Activities*, Milwaukee, Curative Workshop of Milwaukee, 1972.

others. The issue involves the question of independence. Are you more likely to develop a source of career satisfaction by engaging in an independent activity or by developing opportunities to interact and share experiences with others. Neither type has any absolute advantages. The choice depends upon your circumstances and goals. Obviously, you might want to engage in both kinds of activities.

In addition to the independence-dependence idea, there are three other requirements which are useful in selecting new career activities. These are cost, prerequisite conditions, and prerequisite skills.

Cost as a requirement for selecting an activity is, of course, a relative factor. Because our financial resources and our values differ, what seems costly to one person may not to another. The basic point, nevertheless, is to determine the costs involved in an activity before deciding to do it. There are "hidden costs" in some activities which can be significant. Equipment, raw materials, and transportation are examples of costs which may not be obvious at first glance.

Prerequisite conditions necessary to do an activity include, for example, physical facilities (golf courses, skating rinks), geographical features (mountains, lakes, beaches, rivers, woods), and cultural resources (theaters, libraries, educational programs). An otherwise satisfying activity can lead to frustration when the prerequisite conditions are not easily met.

Prerequisite skills simply refer to the idea that more often than not we are most likely to derive satisfaction from an activity for which we possess the "aptitudes" or skills. If, for example, you are "all thumbs" you might think twice before taking up model building or competition sewing. Certainly, skills can be learned, and often the doing of an activity and not the thing it produces is the primary source of satisfaction. You may paint landscapes that would be judged horrible by any standard. So what! As long as you are not looking to the praise of others as the source of satisfaction for the activity, then paint on.

The following list, as indicated earlier, is only a small sample of the huge number of potential activities which can be useful in dealing with no-change career situations. It simply is a way to stimulate your thinking. As other activities occur to you, add them to the list. To the right of the list are three columns, one for each of the three criteria just discussed. As you read the list, you may find it instructive to rate each of the selected activities. The following three-point rating scale can be used.

> 1 = I can meet the requirements for this activity
>
> 2 = I'm not sure whether I can meet the requirements
>
> 3 = I cannot (or choose not to) meet the requirements

You may think of activities about which you lack adequate information regarding costs, conditions, and skills. You can obtain the needed information from libraries, books, and people who are engaged in the activity.

The activities in Table 25 represent just a few of the many, many activities which can serve as a source of satisfaction, anticipation, and purpose when you have decided not to make a relatively major career change. Many of the books reviewed in Chapter 9 describe other activities and identify sources of further information about them.

TABLE 25. Leisure Activities

	COST	CONDITIONS	SKILLS
Games			
Table games			
Darts			
Horseshoes			
Monopoly			
Dice			
Cards			
20 Questions			
Charades			
Jigsaw puzzles			
Crossword puzzles			
Sports			
Sports viewing			
Bicycling			
Rowing			
Sailing			
Ballooning			
Horseback riding			
Jogging			
Skating			
Snorkeling			
Archery			
Bowling			
Lawn bowling			
Golf			
Shooting			

TABLE 25.—*Continued*

	COST	CONDITIONS	SKILLS
Sports *(cont.)*			
Badminton			
Croquet			
Squash			
Table tennis			
Fencing			
Judo			
Volleyball			
Car rallying			
Walking tours			
Nature Activities			
Wildlife observation			
Beachcombing			
Barn viewing			
Wild food gathering			
Camping			
Trapping			
Tropical fish breeding			
Big game hunting			
Outdoor gardening			
Indoor plant raising			
Greenhouse gardening			
Animal care			
Astronomy			
Meterology			
Botany			

TABLE 25.—*Continued*

	COST	CONDITIONS	SKILLS
Nature Activities *(cont.)*			
Conservation—ecology			
Geology			
Rock- and fossil-hunting			
Collecting Activities			
Posters			
Coins			
Fossils			
Rocks			
Models			
Folk art			
Antique books			
Buttons			
Antique bottles			
Recipes			
Blow torch collecting			
Maps			
Photographs (e.g., city halls, airports, amusing signs)			
Crafts			
Cooking			
Sausage-making			
Wine-making			
Gourmet cooking			
Floral arranging			

TABLE 25.—*Continued*

	COST	CONDITIONS	SKILLS
Crafts *(cont.)*			
Quilting			
Furniture			
Rugs			
Kit assembling			
Toy repairing			
Scrapbooks			
Origami			
Bookbinding			
Leather			
Reupholstery			
Whittling			
Soldering and welding			
House decorating			
Appliance repair			
Automobile repair			
Decoupage			
Candlemaking			
Art and Music			
Lettering			
Cartooning			
Wood sculpture			
Joke telling			
Play reading			
Puppet shows			
Ventriloquism			

TABLE 25.—*Continued*

	COST	CONDITIONS	SKILLS
Art and Music *(cont.)*			
Play acting			
Popular dancing			
Square dancing			
Instrument playing			
Group singing			
Letter writing			
Greeting card writing			
Short story writing			
Historical writing			
Film production			
Education, Entertainment, and Cultural Activities			
TV watching, analysis, and evaluation			
TV educational courses			
Movie and theater going			
Reading—general			
Reading—special projects			
Discussion groups			
Group listening			
Attending art festivals			
Special purpose field trips			
Traveling			
Diary keeping			
Churchgoing			

TABLE 25.—*Continued*

	COST	CONDITIONS	SKILLS
Education, Entertainment, and Cultural Activities *(cont.)*			
Individual contemplation			
Religious retreats			
Yoga			
Letter writing			
Figure and weight control			
Poetry writing			
Fiction writing			
Skill improvement courses			
General interest college courses			
Home entertaining			
Going to auctions			
Going to garage sales and flea markets			
Genealogy			
Volunteer Activities			
Professional and managerial assistance			
Library aides			
Museum aides			
Boards of directors			
Stenographic aides			
Reading for the blind			
Blind care			
Foster home management			

TABLE 25.—*Continued*

	COST	CONDITIONS	SKILLS
Volunteer Activities *(cont.)*			
Building maintenance			
Children and youth group services			
Elderly group services			
Sheltered workshop instruction and supervision			
Truck and car driving			
Organizational Activities			
Sports clubs			
Outdoor groups			
Hobby groups			
Game clubs			
Collecting clubs			
Service clubs			
Communication clubs			
Political groups			
Religious groups			
Nonpartisan political and social action groups			
Book clubs			
Ethnic organizations			
Intercultural organizations			
International aid groups			
Investment clubs			
Fraternal organizations			

COPING SKILLS

A second means of dealing with no-change situations is to anticipate the kinds of events or encounters which seem to precipitate dissatisfaction and to predetermine means of coping with them. Some of the procedures discussed in Chapter 7 can be a useful means of coping with sources of dissatisfaction. You can also develop a variety of additional coping skills designed to meet the specifics of a particular situation. In the following paragraphs we have described a relatively simple procedure to help you do just that.

First, identify the general area of career dissatisfaction which is most disconcerting. Then, make a list of situations and events which precipitate dissatisfaction within that area. Be as specific as you can. As a way of reducing the size of the task, review the list and underline those entries which are especially troublesome—those that are either frequent or particularly powerful sources of dissatisfaction.

Now comes the hard part—to think of ways of coping, that is, to identify how you can avoid or reduce the dissatisfaction brought about by a particular kind of event or encounter. There are four means by which coping skills help reduce or avoid dissatisfaction. Most of these skills function as one or more of the following:

- a means of expressing a feeling or thought
- a means of clarifying a situation
- a means of leaving a situation
- a means of restructuring a situation

In attempting to develop a coping skill for a particular situation it is useful to begin by deciding which of the four functions most need to be served. These are examined more carefully in the remaining paragraphs.

Expressing A Feeling Or Thought

Essentially, expressing feelings boils down to how to express them and to whom. The means for expressing them are limited. You can think, speak, write, or express them by some nonverbal behavior. Sometimes merely thinking a thought or feeling is sufficient. Other times it is helpful to actually say it out loud, even to yourself. Saying, "I'm really angry with him," or "I'm feeling sorry for myself again," or "I'm determined to get it done," tends to make the concern more concrete or real. Having said what you are thinking or feeling to yourself can lessen the strength of the dissatisfaction. In other situations, usually when the source of dissatisfaction is more complex or ongoing, writing may be the most effective way to cope. Daily entries in a diary or notebook provide a means for expressing yourself, as well as useful information regarding how you are coping with a situation over a period of time. One mother of three children, for example, who was thoroughly dissatisfied with her role as mediator of her children's seemingly constant arguments, wrote to herself each night before retiring. Initially, the keeping of the diary provided significant relief. She could express the resentment and frustration she felt. As time went by, the entries accumulated. As a result of rereading past entries, she perceived certain patterns and identified the kinds of situations which seemed to precipitate hassles. This, in turn, provided her with a basis for restructuring certain kinds of family interactions, which in turn reduced the number of hassles and, consequently, her own dissatisfaction.

The nonverbal option for expressing feelings and thoughts can take several forms. You can paint, run, swim, build something, or kick a brick, to cite only a few examples. Sometimes this kind of behavior is the most effective means of expression. Some nonverbal behaviors, however, are potentially *more* effective than others. Painting or building something tends to divert your attention from the source of dissatisfaction to a more satisfying activity Kicking a brick, in contrast, tends to maintain attention on the source of dissatisfaction and to place the blame on someone or something besides yourself. That may lead to even more frustration because often there is little we can do to change someone else, and certainly the brick is incapable of rendering much help.

Most people have had the experience of reducing the strength of a feeling or clarifying a thought by talking to another person. "Blowing off steam" and "talking it through" are commonly used coping behaviors. If you have to "get the feeling out" and thinking, speaking, or writing to yourself doesn't suffice, then involving another person may be the best way to cope. The important considerations are the nature of the other person's involvement in your situation and, of course, their willingness to listen. Be careful to whom you express feelings, lest the source of dissatisfaction increases.

Clarifying A Situation

Much of what has just been said regarding expressing feelings also applies to coping with a situation by clarifying what is involved. You can attempt clarification by yourself through thinking, speaking, or writing, or by conferring with another person. In situations where the source of dissatisfaction is with a particular person, you may choose not to use that person as a source of clarification. When you have an unsatisfying relationship with your supervisor, for example, the best policy may not always be a discussion with the supervisor. Being direct, in other words, is not always the best means of clarifying a situation. In this case, conferring with a trusted fellow worker may be more illuminating. On the other hand, many times the most effective and only means of obtaining clarification is to confer directly with those involved. In one family, for example, there was an ongoing disagreement about the time the teenage youngsters were to be home. Curfew hours were constantly set, violated, reset, violated, and reset with arguments between parents and children resulting. The source of parental dissatisfaction was finally diminished as a result of a relatively calm discussion between all concerned. The parents coped with the situation by asking the children to explain why they violated the curfew so often. Did they forget? Not know the time of night? Purposely ignore it? Or what? The discussion made it clear that several things were involved, including the inconsistency with which the curfew hour was set. It seemed to vary each night with the parents' mood. As a result of the discussion, a single week night and a single weekend curfew were established, thus eliminating much of the source of dissatisfaction.

Leaving A Situation

A fairly obvious way to cope with a dissatisfying situation is to leave it. Perhaps equally obvious is the importance of how one leaves. For example, you can leave an argument saying, "Screw you" and stomping out of the room. Or in the same situation one could announce, "I'm getting angry, and thus not much good is coming out of this situation; please try to understand; I'm going to leave before I say things I don't want to say." Smile and then calmly leave and do a couple of laps around the block.

When you know that you may leave a dissatisfying situation, it is often possible to tell others ahead of time. This would reduce the chance of any misunderstandings about your behavior. This may require a little courage, but it could help avoid misunderstandings.

There would seem to be a multitude of dissatisfying situations in which a preannounced, nonoffensive departure would be an effective means of coping. Parents, for example, can cope with meaningless gripe sessions with children by noting, under calmer circumstances, that in the future when pointless arguments begin they intend to leave the room. It is also likely that most post-party marital arguments could be avoided if the couple agreed ahead of time that if an intolerable situation developed, one or both would leave. The chief risk to this course of action is that others may not "like" us as a result of our leaving. Often, however, they may like us even less, and we they, if we don't leave.

Finally, in regard to leaving as a means of coping, it isn't always necessary to physically displace your body. Daydreaming, thinking about another issue, or even a short fantasy trip are coping behaviors which most of us have used at one time or another to "leave" a situation.

Restructuring Situations

In many situations coping with sources of dissatisfaction can be achieved by restructuring. Restructuring can involve social considerations, such as changing the rules of interaction; psychological considerations, such as altering your perception; and physical considerations, such as rearranging facilities. Probably the only limit to coping with situations by restructuring them is your imagination. Thus, if we can simply suggest the various uses of restructuring, our objective will have been met.

One obvious means of social restructuring is to simply leave a situation, as pointed out above. When this cannot be done and you find it necessary or desirable to engage in dissatisfying situations, restructuring your social behavior can be helpful. For example, even though you have to go to a dreadful social engagement, you do have some control over the people with whom you interact. You can also be selective about the people with whom you spend time on the job. You can, in other words, overcome social and institutional mores which result in your doing things that you would rather not do.

The key to effective restructuring of social situations is thinking ahead or anticipating the dissatisfying situations, and planning new ways of behaving. By doing so you are less likely to get caught up in the kinds of interactions which precipitate dissatisfaction. One salesman, for example, had a colleague who habitually dropped by his office every Monday morning. The colleague's intent was simply to be friendly, but he usually remained for nearly an hour and thus kept the salesman from important tasks. As a means of coping with the situation, the salesman instructed his secretary to begin placing the morning's phone calls about ten minutes after the colleague arrived. The first week that this procedure was followed the colleague patiently sat through most of the phone conversations. Within a couple of weeks, however, his impatience got the best of him and thereafter he left as each week's initial phone call came in.

Psychological restructuring is essentially a matter of changing your perception of a situation. The concept was illustrated in Chapter 5 by the discussion about analyzing constraints. There, it will be recalled, we described a procedure for changing statements of the form "I cannot do A because of B" to the form "If I do A then B must be dealt with." The underlying concept, as noted earlier, is perceiving your dissatisfaction as your own responsibility or problem, and not that of someone or something else. If the change in perception is actually effected, then you are more likely to either do something about the situation (because it is now your responsibility) or decide that tolerating it is preferable to doing something to change it. Another aspect of psychological restructuring via perception is being sure that you are not over-generalizing. For example, one student had an unpleasant math teacher and to make matters worse, math was the student's poorest subject. As a result, the student was reminded each math period that he was a stupid lunkhead. The student gradually became depressed, discouraged, and developed a generally negative self-image. A counselor helped him solve his problem by encouraging him to review his perceptions of the situation. The student had been saying to himself, "I'm not worth much; people think I'm stupid." After reviewing his perceptions, he was able to more accurately say to himself "One person I come in contact with thinks I'm stupid, but I don't get that reaction from anyone else. I wish that I could do better in math and that I had a more understanding teacher. But that's only a small part of an otherwise enjoyable life."

The final kind of coping via restructuring involves rearranging your physical environment in one manner or another. For example, one family was suddenly confronted with the fact that the mother was to be confined to a wheelchair. In addition to reassigning many responsibilities, the family coped with the situation by lowering work surfaces and appliances in the kitchen. Another family who faced living in a much overcrowded apartment for a year decided to store all but their essential pieces of furniture. They did without things they enjoyed, but they created the much needed space.

Other types of environmental restructuring such as reassigning children's bedrooms, changing transportation arrangements, changing meal schedules, and reallocating family spending priorities can be effective means of coping with dissatisfying situations.

You may now want to review the list of dissatisfying events and situations we suggested you make. Think through each situation and ask yourself if each of the four kinds of coping skills apply. When a type of coping skill seems relevant, imagine how you might use it when that situation reappears. The procedures described in Chapter 7 also can be helpful as a means of developing new coping behaviors.

MAXIMIZING CURRENT SOURCES OF SATISFACTION

Finally, there is an obvious, but often overlooked, strategy for dealing with no-change career situations, and that is to increase the satisfaction derived from pleasurable ongoing activities. The strategy involves finding ways to extend an activity so that it involves other people, or in some other manner offers greater stimulation, challenge, or substance. The following examples may stimulate you to think of ways of using this particular kind of strategy in a no-change situation.

Herman disliked his job, but for several reasons decided that a job change was not desirable at this time. Nevertheless he believed that for the sake of his own mental health he needed to identify some means of increasing career satisfaction. In thinking about his current situation, he realized that his chief source of satisfaction was "tinkering." Each week he spent some time fixing his car or repairing some other mechanical device. He seldom planned these activities, but simply drifted into one after another. A major void in tinkering, he realized, was the lack of interaction with other people. Tinkering was a solitary activity. After making a few inquiries at local garages, Herman learned of an informal group of people who worked together restoring old automobiles. He contacted one member of the group and discovered that they would welcome his help. As a result, he expanded his "tinkering" into a major source of career satisfaction which could be shared with other people.

Expanding a solitary activity to include group contact is an obvious and often easy means of increasing the satisfaction you can derive from it. Depending upon the size of the population where we live, there are groups interested in everything from antelope hunting to zigzag stitchery. Even when groups do not exist locally, many share-by-mail opportunities can be found. Craft, hobby, and other special interest magazines are useful for identifying such opportunities.

When increased personal interaction is not important, there are other ways of maximizing existing sources of career satisfaction.

One person who gained some satisfaction from collecting stamps, increased the value of this activity by specializing in selected kinds of stamps and increasing the amount of background reading regarding his collection. Another, who enjoyed reading travel magazines, gained more from the activity by initiating correspondence with individuals and organizations spotted in his readings. A woman who enjoyed looking at antique furniture increased her satisfaction by expanding her interest to restoring selected pieces. A salesman who enjoyed occasional photography expanded his satisfaction by taking his camera along on business trips and starting a collection of photographs of old barns.

As we indicated, the point seems obvious but often overlooked. Many of us have sources of career satisfaction which can be expanded and increased when a no-change situation exists.

In this chapter we have suggested that even in situations where you decide not to make a relatively major career change, all hope need not be abandoned. Three ways of improving no-change career change situations were described. They include initiating minor new activities; developing procedures to cope with circumstances which precipitate dissatisfaction; and maximizing current sources of satisfaction.

chapter 9

Career Information

In this chapter we turn to the third kind of career change competency—information. More specifically, our concern is sources of career information. This chapter is essentially an annotated bibliography of books and directories which we have found particularly useful to those contemplating career change. The descriptions are grouped under the following categories:

Educational Opportunities and Plans
>   Four-Year Colleges and Universities
>   >   General Information
>   >   College Admissions Testing
>   >   Selection Services
>   Two-Year Colleges and Schools
>   Occupational Education

Financial

Leisure

Marriage

Occupational Plans and Opportunities
>   Career Planning
>   Job Hunting
>   Women
>   International
>   Researching Aids

Parent-Child Problems

Retirement

Only a small sampling of the large number of books regarding various careers are included. Your library and bookstore will have many others. As we hope you are by now convinced, none of the books contain "the answer." They do, however, contain facts, ideas, and descriptions which should be useful as you proceed with the process of making your own career change decisions and plans.

Perhaps 75 percent of the books described are relatively inexpensive paperbacks. Books which are library references are indicated by an asterisk (*).

EDUCATIONAL OPPORTUNITIES AND PLANS

Four-Year Colleges and Universities

General Information

* *The College Blue Book,* 10 vols. New York: CCM Information Corporation, latest edition. This is probably the most comprehensive and detailed educational directory available. The content of each volume is summarized below. The summaries are excerpted from Volume 4.

Volume 1: *Guide and Index to College Blue Book*

The section, "How to Use the College Blue Book," includes the new Student Form for College Selection, as well as guidelines for selecting a college and planning for it. There are complete instructions on how-to-use for each volume in this section.

The section, "Special Lists of Colleges," includes lists of colleges accepting "C" students; predominantly black colleges; women's colleges; men's colleges; two-year colleges; and colleges offering ROTC.

Analytical Index to all volumes of CBB, in alphabetical order.

Volume 2: *U.S. Colleges: Tabular Data*

Over 3,400 U.S. colleges are listed alphabetically by state, in an easy-to-read, two-color tabular format. Information about entrance requirements, costs, accreditation, enrollment figures, faculty, location, year founded, ROTC, and the names of the chief administrative officer and registrar is given for each school. Each of the 3,400 institutions has a unique number which ties it to the narrative description given in Volume 3.

Volume 3: *U.S. Colleges: Narrative Descriptions*

Each of the 3,400 colleges listed in Volume 2 is fully described in Volume 3. Exact procedures are given for filing admission applications, and campus facilities are discussed.

Volume 4: *Degrees Offered, by Subject*

Over 2,100 subject areas for which degrees are granted by one or more institutions of higher education are listed in alphabetical order. Colleges offering degrees in each subject are listed in state order.

Volume 5: *Degrees Offered, by College*

Each of the more than 3,400 colleges listed in volumes 2 and 3 appears in Volume 5, in alphabetical order by state. Under the name of each college appears a list of the subject areas for which they offer degrees.

Volume 6: *College Atlas*

This volume describes the geographical location of each of the schools listed in volumes 2 and 3. Airline routes, bus and train schedules, as well as highway information, are given for each town. In addition, a full-page map of each state identifies the location of all colleges within the state.

Volume 7: *Specialized Educational Programs*

This volume offers information about many educational opportunities available in the U.S. and abroad. Associated institutions of higher education are listed and described; complete information on church-related colleges and universities is given; general information regarding accredited schools and courses offered through the National Home Study Council is given. Correspondence courses offered by institutions that are affiliated with the National University Extension Association are listed.

In a separate section called Study Abroad, there is complete information about enrollment, curricula, and tuition for most of the major universities abroad.

Volume 8: *Professions, Careers, and Accreditation*

The first section of this volume, "Choosing a Career," defines and identifies professions and careers likely to be of greatest interest to *College Blue Book* users. Accreditation associations are listed, together with the schools that are accredited by each organization. In addition, professional and educational associations related to the professions listed earlier in the volume are listed and described.

Volume 9: *Scholarships, Fellowships, and Grants*

This volume lists over $1 million in available scholarships, together with information about when and how to apply and who is eligible.

Volume 10: *Secondary Schools in the U.S.*

Over 30,000 junior and senior high schools in the U.S are listed with information about type of school and accreditation. In addition, separate lists of parochial and private schools are given.

* *The College Handbook,* New York: College Entrance Examination Board, current edition. Describes each of the colleges which are affiliated with College Entrance Examination Board. Written for the potential student with his questions in mind.

College Admissions Testing

American College Testing Program

College Entrance Examination Board

Many colleges require students to take the examinations of one of these organizations as part of their admission procedure. The tests are given several times each year on specified dates. School counselors have the testing schedules and application materials for both programs.

Selection Services

Several college admission services are available for students who may have some difficulty gaining college admission and who wish to have their credentials considered by a number of accredited colleges. Two such services are:

The College Admission Service
610 Church St.
Evanston, Illinois 60201

College Admission Center
41 East 65th St.
New York, New York 10021

Two-Year Colleges and Schools

* Campbell, Gordon, *Community College in Canada.* Toronto/New York/ London: Ryerson Press, 1971.

Brief descriptions of Canadian community colleges listed by province. Includes academic, financial, and admission information.

* Cass, James and Bernbaum, *Comparative Guide to Two-Year Colleges and Four-Year Specialized Schools and Programs.* New York: Harper and Row, 1969.

Brief listing of many community colleges. Special value is its emphasis on colleges offering programs in the performing arts including art, dance, music, theater, radio-TV, and film.

* Gleazer, Edmond J., ed., *American Junior Colleges,* 8th ed., Washington, D.C.: American Council on Education.

Sponsored by the American Council on Education and the American Association of Junior Colleges, this volume describes all two-year institutions accredited by nationally recognized accrediting agencies. Covers all states and territories and lists public and private institutions separately. There is also a listing of two-year institutions according to the programs offered in various occupational fields.

Occupational Education

* Miller, A. E., and Brown, B. I. *National Directory of Schools and Vocations.* No. Springfield, Pa.: State School Publications, 1967.

Lists colleges according to occupation programs from "accountant to x-ray clerk." An initial reference, little descriptive information.

* Russell, Max W., ed., *The Blue Book of Occupational Education,* New York: CCM Corp., 1971.

Presents information on nearly 12,000 occupational schools in the United States. Describes schools and indexes by programs of instruction offered from accounting to zinc platemaking. The main headings from the table of contents suggest the scope of the book. These are:

Occupational Schools of the United States

Curricula and Programs of Instruction

Accredited Business Schools

Two-Year Institutions of the United States

Accredited Home Study Schools

Schools Offering Two-Year Library Technology Programs

Accredited Medical and Dental Technological Schools
of the United States

Nursing Schools of the United States

Schools Approved for Veteran's Training

Apprenticeship Training

United States Occupational Training Programs

Guide to Nation's Job Openings

Financial Aid

Sources of Additional Information

FINANCIAL

Callenbach, Ernest. *Living Poor With Style*. New York: Bantam Books, 1972.

For those who want advice on saving money *Living Poor With Style* is a must. There are a multitude of suggestions regarding expenditures for food, shelter, transportation, furnishings, clothing, medical services, recreation, education and training, and raising children. This advice is laced with comments about governmental policy and social issues. There is a definite bias: it is "in" to be poor and against the mainstream culture. Aware of this, readers can objectively read the ideas and useful hints and judge whether they can use them in their own life-style.

Crook De Camp, Catherine. *The Money Tree*. New York: New American Library, 1972.

This book is useful for those who need general information in many financial areas. After reading the book, one inexperienced in money matters should feel more confident.

The book begins with an elementary discussion of assets and liabilities and suggestions for developing a spending plan. Comparative government data on family spending are given. Methods for the art and discipline of record keeping are discussed, and illustrative forms are displayed in the appendix.

Helpful chapters are included on credit buying; building or buying/renting a home; buying a car; and financing a car. In each of these chapters specific information is given regarding who to see, what to look for, and what to compare. Other chapters are included on shopping skills and common fraudulent business practices.

The author also deals with the issues of saving, stocks, and Social Security. The appendix includes a good bibliography.

Ferguson, Marilyn and Mike. *Champagne Living on a Beer Budget*. New York: Berkley Publishing Corporation, 1973.

The usual topics on consuming or spending wisely in the areas of food, housing, furnishings, clothing, transportation, babies, medicine, gift-giving, recreation, travel, and government benefits are treated. Other topics, not usually treated in similar books, include how-to information for saving on telephone rates, stating consumer complaints, investing money, renting almost anything, and planning efficiently.

The writing style of this book makes it particularly interesting and useful. Each chapter includes anecdotes and specific suggestions.

Halcomb, Ruth. *Money and the Working Ms.* Chatsworth, Calif.: Books for Better Living, 1974.

This book is designed to assist the single working woman do effective financial planning. The author, a single working mother, states that the book's purpose is "to help you initiate a total program for wise spending and saving."

After describing case studies of ineffective women spenders, the author urges the reader to make a master plan complete with goals and a careful study of one's assets and liabilities. The next step is to develop a workable budget. The items of most budgets—food, shelter, furnishings, clothes, entertainment, transportation—are specifically discussed in subsequent chapters, and guidelines are presented for determining the priorities within.

Other financial concerns such as dealing with emergencies and taxes are also discussed. A special chapter discusses economic and psychological problems in raising children alone.

The book concludes with a brief discussion of investment possibilities for the single woman.

The Mother Earth News Almanac. New York: Bantam Books, 1973.

All those interested in a book chock-full of ideas and helpful hints from A to Z will enjoy *The Mother Earth News Almanac*. This 361-page almanac has literally thousands of practical suggestions and how-to information. These include ideas which are:

Practical (how to make a compost)

Fun (building a kite)

Old-timey (folk medicine)

Designed for those wanting to get "back to the land" (tips on raising animals)

Helpful in improving city and suburban life (how to grow a sprout garden in a closet)

Futuristic (using solar energy for heating homes)

A number of the ideas enumerated can save the reader money. A good book for a rainy afternoon, and one you will use as a ready reference thereafter.

Poriss, Martin. *How to Live Cheap But Good*. New York: Dell Publishing Co., Inc., 1971.

This book is primarily geared to the apartment dweller and college student but because of the variety and clarity of money-saving hints it is recommended for others as well. The six chapters include the following:

Home Is Where You Find It

- Includes hints on how to find and select the best living unit for you.
- Deals with signing a lease.
- Has apartment hunter's checklist.

A Moving Experience

- Includes a step-by-step procedure for moving your possessions.

Shoveling Out, Fixing Up, and Furnishing

- Specific advice on cleaning and fixing one's home and furnishings.

Thought for Food

- Information ranges from what kind of equipment should be in the kitchen to how one should buy fruits and vegetables and cooking methods and techniques.

Home Repairs for the Poet

- Step-by-step procedures for repairing plumbing, electrical fixtures, doors, windows, and radiators.

Getting Your Money's Worth

- Includes ideas for saving on clothes, health care, and utility bills as well as how to be an effective consumer.

Scaduto, Anthony. *Getting the Most for Your Money*. New York: Paperback Library, 1970.

A real gem for general consumer information—such as skills for wise shopping and charts showing which months different items (e.g. appliances, clothing, cars, etc.) are most likely to be on sale. The book deals in depth with major spending items. Chapters are included on:

- Buying food
- Buying clothes
- Household appliance purchases

- Buying and maintaining a car
- Recreational spending
- Financing college educations
- Buying property and life insurance
- Medical expenses

Each chapter provides specific facts, information, or shopping hints for making the most of your dollar. (For example, the chapter on buying food provides general food-buying hints and specific buying tips for meat, dairy products, baked goods, etc.)

The chapter on financing a college education asked the reader to complete a worksheet estimating and comparing expenses at the different colleges being considered. It describes the financial options available (student employment, loans, scholarships, and grants) and lists where to write for more information.

Shortney, Joan Ranson. *How to Live on Nothing*. New York: Pocket Books, 1973.

Highly recommended by *The Whole Earth Catalogue* for its practical and accurate information; this 320-page book suggests how to save money on the following topics: food, clothing, household furnishings, buying a house, maintenance and repair work, heating your house, gift-giving, vacationing, medicine, and knowing your social benefits. Information is thorough on each topic, and the reader is usually provided instructions for researching the topics discussed. Sometimes the reader is provided an inexpensive source of further information, such as a government publication.

The last chapter of the book consists of a list of 100 usually discarded objects and ways to reuse them. The good life, suggests the author, can be found by using the skills found in this book.

LEISURE

Lowery, Lucie. *Your Leisure Time . . . How to Enjoy It*. Los Angeles: Ward Richie Press, 1972.

Intended for those who live in the Los Angeles area, the book is also a useful guide for those living in other geographical areas. Following a brief discussion of the current status of leisure time, are seven chapters on various areas of leisure. Topics include high-risk leisure pursuits, artistic pursuits, scientific hobbies, physical activities, intellectual activities, volunteer activities, and offbeat leisure activities. Each chapter is punctuated with interesting stories about people who engage in the leisure activities discussed.

A "fun test" gives the reader his "leisure quotient." The book concludes with a list of people and organizations in the Los Angeles area which can assist in fulfilling one's leisure needs.

* Overs, Robert; O'Connor, Elizabeth; DeMarco, Barbara. *Guide to Avocational Activities*. Milwaukee, Wis.: Curative Workshop of Milwaukee, 1972.

This is a three-volume study which has provided a classification system for leisure activities. The system uses the following nine categories:

Games

Sports

Nature Activities

Collection Activities

Craft Activities

Art and Music Activities

Education, Entertainment, and Cultural Activities

Volunteer Activities

Organizational Activities

There are literally hundreds of activities briefly described in the three volumes. In addition to the description, each activity is rated according to environmental, social-psychological, and cost factors. Of special interest to some readers is an indication of the extent to which various kinds of physical impairments limit doing each activity.

Yee, Min S., ed. *The Great Escape*. New York: Bantam Books, 1974.

This very intriguing book is subtitled "A Source Book of Delights and Pleasures for the Mind and Body." It is a compilation of facts, information, and ideas on how to escape from the ordinary. The book is loosely organized into the following escape areas. Just a sample of the escapes are noted:

- Mind and body (martial arts, belly dancing, the occult)
- Water (white-water rafting, sand trekking, swamp buggies)
- Land (hikes, gold fever, skiing)

- Nomadics (free travel, flying by thumb)
- Places (ethnic places, U.S.A., country auctions)
- Games (computer games, unusual games)

Each article gives enough description to hook the reader and enough information to get you to the next resource.

MARRIAGE

Bach, George R., and Deutsch, Ronald M. *Pairing: How to Achieve Genuine Intimacy*. New York: Avon Books, 1970.

Dr. Bach, the author of *The Intimate Enemy,* has essentially outlined the same type of techniques as in his first book. The techniques, developed and used at The Institute of Group Psychotherapy, rely heavily on the expression of feelings in the here-and-now. Some of the techniques may appear rather "gimmicky." There are several useful suggestions and guidelines for effective communication procedures. The authors have coined many words to describe "bad" non-intimate behaviors (gunnysacking, mind-raping, thingin) and "correct" intimate behaviors (leveling, meditation) which at times detract from the instruction value of the book because one is "caught up" in lingo. The book does succeed in demonstrating that we often misread an intimate and that the use of some fairly basic communication procedures can produce mutually satisfying results.

Baer, Jean. *The Second Wife*. New York: Pyramid Books, 1973.

In today's society many women will face the issues involved in marrying a man who has already made marriage vows before. This book outlines problems involved and discusses alternative solutions. Based on 220 interviews with second wives the situations discussed include:

- How to be a weekend stepmother
- How to be a full-time mother for his, mine, and ours
- How to deal with the legal and financial realities of the situation
- How to deal with the ex-wife in a variety of circumstances.

The book concludes by discussing why many second marriages fail. This is a useful book for those who are in or who contemplate entering a second marriage situation.

Bernard, Jessie. *The Future of Marriage*. New York: Bantam Books, Inc., 1972.

A very readable, but academic view of the past, present, and future of marriage. The author, a sociologist, has written a number of other books including *The Sex Game* and *The Academic Woman*.

When discussing the future of marriage, it is important to state whose marriage is being discussed—the husband's or the wife's. Considerable research shows that there are, in fact, two marriages in each union; and they often do not coincide.

After an interesting discussion of the history and current status of marriage, the author presents some other male and female writers' options for the future of marriage. These range from celibacy to communal neighborhoods. The author's own view is that marriage does have a future—a future of many options. These options will create many new demands, but the author does not state that the marriage partners will be happier or better adjusted than currently. She ends by making a plea to upgrade the wife's marriage.

Knox, David. *Marriage Happiness: A Behavioral Approach to Counseling*. Champaign, Ill.: Research Press, 1972.

This book is recommended to those who are considering marriage counseling which employs a behavioral approach. For some people this approach makes a great deal of sense, and reading this book can prepare them for the relatively prescriptive techniques that will be utilized.

The first portion provides a general discussion of marital behavior. The underlying concept is that if the outcome (result) of the behavior is negative, the spouse is *less* likely to repeat it. If the outcome is positive, the spouse will more likely repeat it. Changing behavior then is the name of the game. The author outlines several techniques to change behavior, and describes how they can be used to resolve marital problems.

The author also devotes a chapter to each of the following marital problems: sex, communication, alcohol, in-laws, friends, religion, money, recreation, and children. The format in each of these chapters is similar. The author describes how behavioral techniques can be utilized to deal with the various problems.

The last section of the book is devoted to case studies from the author's experiences.

Lederer, William J., and Jackson, Don D. *The Mirages of Marriage*. New York: W. W. Norton and Company, Inc., 1968.

The Mirages of Marriage discusses marriage as it is, not as the romantics would realize it. After a brief description of the history of marriage, many of the false assumptions of modern marriage are identified. For example, the authors state that one false assumption is that loneliness will be cured by marriage.

Marriage is described as an interlocking system. The behavior of one spouse creates a reaction from the other spouse. At many times the behavior of one spouse conflicts with what the other desires (e.g., disagreement on which TV show to watch, where to go on a vacation, or how to spend a bonus). Specific techniques and exercises to train couples to negotiate are outlined.

The book also contains a marital checklist and a discussion on the use of marital counselors.

Lobsenz, Norman M., and Blackburn, Clark W. *How to Stay Married*. Greenwick, Conn.: Fawcett Publications, Inc., 1969.

Two particularly valuable aspects of this book are: (1) the "no nonsense" approach to marriage that is illustrated, and (2) a presentation of the viewpoint and philosophy of the Family Service Association.

In regard to the first aspect, the book is believable—it tells it like it is. This is achieved in part, by the inclusion of examples of problems common to most marriages. In all of the topics dealt with such as in-laws, first adjustments, sex, money, communications, and role expectations, the authors give examples or case studies of the problem and offer general guidelines for solutions. No "cure all," but a readable, intelligent approach.

The second value of the book—acquainting one with the philosophy of Family Service—is important to any couple contemplating using that service. A list of all the Family Service Associations by state is included.

O'Neill, Nena, and O'Neill, George. *Open Marriage*. New York: Avon Books, 1973.

According to the authors, "open marriage means an honest and open relationship between two people, based on the equal freedom and identity of both partners. It involves a verbal, intellectual, and emotional commitment to the right of each to grow as an individual within the marriage." The authors identify eight cardinal guidelines to achieving an open marriage. These are:

- Living for Now and Realistic Expectations
- Privacy
- Open and Honest Communication
- Flexibility in Roles
- Open Companionship
- Equality
- Identity
- Trust

The core of the book outlines methods for following the guidelines. The authors contend that achieving an open marriage is a "self-reinforcing, regenerative, and growth-enhancing system" that continues to expand.

Steinor, Bernard. *When Parents Divorce*. New York: Pocket Books, 1970.

The author's contention is that parents as well as children can grow emotionally through the process of divorce. He further believes that "the friendly divorce" recommended by many is not always the best option because it can lead to hypocrisy and phoniness. Instead, he proposes a psychological divorce or "divorce with freedom" that legitimately recognizes the differences between the parting couple.

This book is most useful to those contemplating divorce, not because it gives the "right" answers but because it points up many of the issues which divorcing couples with children must face. Issues discussed include: reaching agreements on custody and property, telling the children about the divorce, problems of the custodial parent and the visitation parent, and considering dating and remarriage. The author advises that these issues be dealt with honestly and gives many specific examples of the problems that can arise within them.

OCCUPATIONAL PLANS AND OPPORTUNITIES

Career Planning

Beitz, Charles, and Washburn, Michael *Creating the Future*. New York: Bantam Books, 1974.

Subtitled "A Guide to Living and Working for Social Change," the book is a very useful resource for those with such aspirations. The author claims that people can work for social change both within established institutions or through creating alternative institutions. An introductory section describes idealized communities in terms of services and governmental operations. Major concern is with specific areas of social change and how to find out more about these areas. Included are chapters on media, education, health, business, politics, science and technology, church, labor, and the federal government. Each chapter outlines social change possibilities and concludes with extensive resource lists of people, places, or things to contact for further information. If social change is your thing, this is a good buy!

Biggs, Don. *Breaking Out . . . of a Job You Don't Like . . . and the Regimented Life*. New York: David McKay Co., Inc., 1973.

This chronicles the dissatisfactions with the corporate life and gives many case histories of people, primarily men, who have left their high-salaried jobs. Two chapters are concerned with practical aspects of the situation. One problem is how to deal with less income; another chapter discusses what corporations can do to try to alleviate the situation.

Carnegie Commission on Higher Education. *College Graduates and Jobs*. New York: McGraw-Hill Book Co., 1973.

This report, prepared by the Carnegie Commission on Higher Education, gives an updated and projected view of employment for the college graduate. The report outlines the changes in the job market from 1900–1970, and then projects the outlook for college graduates in the 70s. Projections in the specific fields of teaching, health, law, business administration, engineering, and science are included. Another chapter is devoted to the changing market for the Ph.D. The recommendations of the Commission are interspersed throughout the report.

* *Dictionary of Occupational Titles, Vol. I, Definitions of Titles*. Washington, D.C.: U.S. Government Printing Office, 1965.

Volume I of the *Dictionary of Occupational Titles*, has definitions of 35,500 job titles arranged alphabetically. The definitions are short (10–15 lines) and specific about job duties and responsibilities. This is the basic reference in occupational information.

Dunphy, Philip W., ed., *Career Development for the College Student*. Cranston, R.I.: Carroll Press, 1969.

Section One, "Career Theory," and Section Three, "Techniques for Career Implementation," are the most useful parts of this publication. Section Two, "Areas of Opportunities," is available in more recent publications. Sample resumes, cover letters, and additional letters are described.

* Forrester, Gertrude. *Occupational Literature: An Annotated Bibliography*. Bronx, N.Y.: The H. W. Wilson Company, 1971.

A reference book to use in your local library for finding sources of information on specific occupations. Most of this 600-page volume is an annotated bibliography of books and pamphlets describing occupations. Occupations are listed alphabetically starting with Able Seaman and ending with Zoologist. Under Zoologist, for example, ten books and pamphlets are listed (prices included). Addresses of all publishers listed are included.

Various specialized bibliographies include: job-seeking, occupations for the handicapped, planning a career, scholarships, professional counseling services, apprenticeships, foreign study, and employment.

The Graduate. Knoxville, Tenn.: Approach 13–30 Corporation, 1973.

An annual magazine for graduating college seniors subtitled "A Handbook for Leaving School." Using the style and format of newsstand publications, the brochure has more visual appeal than many other publications dealing with similar information.

Topics range from job outlooks to issues faced by minority graduates to a special section on "The Real World Catalog." The latter section covers such items as arranging your finances, insurance, costs of moving, buying a stereo, and other "real world" facts. A helpful publication for the soon-to-be graduate.

Hecht, Miriam, and Traub, Lillian. *Alternatives to College*. New York: Macmillan Publishing Co., 1974.

A guide to the alternatives without a 4-year degree. After an introductory section on knowing yourself, the following alternatives are considered: occupational education, apprenticeships, learning to type, starting your own business, volunteer work, the armed forces, and combination packages.

* Hopke, William, ed., *The Encyclopedia of Careers and Vocational Guidance,* Vol. 2. Chicago: Ferguson Publishing Co., 1972.

The feature which makes these volumes valuable is combining interesting and readable articles by national leaders in a wide variety of industries with specific data on salaries, educational requirements, numbers employed, and advancement possibilities for over 650 occupations. Some information is duplicated in *Occupational Outlook Handbook* and some is new.

Joseph, James. *The Complete Out-of-Doors Job, Business and Profession Guide.* Chicago: Henry Regnery Co., 1974.

The cover states that this is "a career guide for those ready to trade urban sprawl, pollution, high taxes, and growing crime rates for a personally fulfilling, financially rewarding life out-of-doors." The book is organized into 50 chapters that describe a range of opportunities in the out-of-doors. Information is included on qualifications or skills needed, earnings, employment outlook, where to write for more information, and selected references.

Loughary, John W., and Ripley, Theresa M. *This Isn't Quite What I Had in Mind.* Eugene, Ore.: United Learning Corporation, 1974.

An exercise book for assessing self awareness of skills, abilities, values, needs, and decision-making for individualizing goals and objectives in career planning. The last part of the book has an extensive bibliography of publications pertinent to job hunting, resume writing, and career change information.

Lakein, Alan. *How to Get Control of Your Time and Your Life.* New York: The New American Library, Inc., 1973.

Mr. Lakein's purpose is to teach the reader how to set goals and then how to achieve those goals for effectively using your time. In the first portion of the book specific exercises assist the reader to set lifetime and shorter-term goals. Scheduling and planning your time is encouraged and specific techniques for doing so are outlined. Not all of these ideas will appeal to everyone, but the author has decided to give several techniques so you can choose which ones might work for you.

McKee, Bill. *New Careers for Teachers*. Chicago: Henry Regnery Company, 1972.

For a variety of reasons fewer positions are currently available for teachers. This book is intended to assist teachers find positions in teaching and non-teaching fields. The publication is divided into four sections:

I. A self evaluation of interests, aptitudes, experience, and knowledge

II. Descriptions of jobs for which little or no re-training would be necessary

III. The nitty gritty of getting a job—resumes and interviews

IV. Nontraditional careers in education

A good place to start for teachers who find they must (or want) to make a career change.

O'Neill, Nena, and O'Neill, George. *Shifting Gears*. New York: M. Evans & Co., Inc., 1974.

The O'Neills have written a book that helps an adult think about mid-life career crisis or change from a different perspective. In essence they reaffirm that it's alright if you feel frustrated, slightly confused, and unfulfilled if you are at mid-age and from society's viewpoint "have it made."

They state that "shifting gears" consists of the following steps:

- awareness
- evaluation
- exploration
- experimentation
- decision
- commitment to action
- letting go

One strength of the book is the number of real-life examples given of people facing and going through the "shifting gears" process.

* *Occupational Outlook Handbook*. Washington, D.C.: U. S. Government Printing Office. Published biannually.

A reference available in most public libraries. More than 800 occupations are discussed. Each individual occupational listing describes the nature of the work, places of employment, training, other qualifications, advancement opportunities, employment outlook, earnings, and working conditions. Places to write for additional information are included at the end of each description. This reference is useful for all educational and age levels.

Richmond, Adrianne. *New Careers for Social Workers*. Chicago: Henry Regnery Company, 1974.

More than 100 non-social work occupations that require nominal as well as considerable additional training are listed; also includes federal government and self-employment possibilities as well as paraprofessional fields, and business and communications areas.

Robertson, Laura. *How to Start a Money-Making Business at Home*. New York: Frederick Fell Publishers, Inc., 1969.

This book is an initial aid for those who want to go into business for themselves. It is a source of ideas regarding a number of small business ventures that are service-oriented. Each chapter describes a service and briefly suggests how to get organized and started, and gives information on initial operating expenses. Some of the services described include: 24-hour dictation and transportation service, art rental agencies, personal shopping services, handicraft associations, and dressmaking services.

Splaver, Sarah. *Paraprofessions*. New York: Julian Messner, 1974.

Discusses career opportunities of the future and the present on the paraprofession or helping professional level; includes a section on where to write for further information.

* Teal, Everett A. *The Occupational Thesaurus* 2 vols. Bethlehem, Penn.: Lehigh University, 1971.

This reference set is designed to assist the reader in learning the job opportunities which exist for particular college majors. The following majors are included: anthropology, economics, history, languages, mathematics, political science, psychology, sociology, accounting, biology, chemistry, finance, geology, management, marketing, physics, and transportation.

Entry occupations are listed for each of these major fields of study. The effect, particularly for the reader in liberal arts, is the realization that many options are available with an undergraduate degree.

* *Vocational Biographies.* Sauk Centre, Minn.: Vocational Biographies, 1972.

The *Vocational Biographies* series is a helpful tool in career planning. Each series contains 6 volumes, and each volume has twenty-five four-page case histories describing the careers of people in the vocations spotlighted. Biographies conclude with specific job facts and places to write for further information.

The strength of *Vocational Biographies* is that the information is presented in an interesting, involving manner. Blue collar as well as white collar occupations are included.

Job Hunting

Bolles, Richard Nelson. *What Color Is Your Parachute?* Berkeley, Calif.: Ten Speed Press, 1973.

Subtitled, "A Practical Manual for Job-hunters and Career Changers," the book begins by describing why traditional strategies for job search are ineffective. The author discourages what he calls "the numbers game" approach to job hunting (e.g., sending out 100 resumes to get six job interviews).

Bolles' three-step prescription for job search consists of:

1. Deciding "just exactly what you want to do."
2. Deciding "just exactly where you want to do it, through your own research and personal survey."
3. "Researching the organizations that interest you at great length, and then approaching the one individual in each organization who has the power to hire you for the job that you have decided you want to do."

The remainder of the book describes exactly how to complete these three steps. This is one of the better how-to books on job searching.

Irish, Richard K. *Go Hire Yourself an Employer.* Garden City, N.Y.: Anchor Books, 1973.

A question-and-answer format is used in this how-to-do-a-job-search book. Traditional strategies of completing resumes and setting goals are covered. The author also makes the point that you, the employee, are really hiring an employer and thus it is up to you to interview the interviewer and negotiate your salary. Outlines for implementing this strategy are presented.

The last two chapters of the book deal with special employment situations (being a CO, a woman, a minority, handicapped) and opportunities with the federal government.

Jacquish, Michael P. *Personal Resume Preparation*. New York: John Wiley and Sons, Inc., 1968.

An excellent guide for resume preparation. The case for an effective resume is made clearly. Four resume formats are clearly discussed and illustrated (chronological, functional, organizational, and creative). The reader is helped to assess which is best for his/her particular situation. Several suggestions are given for dealing with sometimes "sticky" issues such as, reason for leaving last position, age, desired salary, and marital status. Clear, concise information and illustrations are given on such considerations as the actual typing, paper, and printing specifications for the resume. The last chapter details guidelines to use when writing cover letters. Examples of cover letters are included.

Lukowski, Susan; and Piton, Margaret. *Strategies and Tactics for Getting a Government Job*. Washington, D.C.: Potomac Books, Inc., 1972.

This "how-to" publication on the ins and outs of federal service focuses on being hired in Washington, D.C., and is written from the first-hand experiences of the authors. The information includes election campaigns, summer jobs, internships, overseas, foreign language, private industry, executive department identification and addresses as well as independent agency addresses in Washington, D.C. and regional U.S.A.

Nutter, Carolyn F. *The Resume Workbook*. Cranston, R.I.: Carroll Press, 1970.

As the title indicates, the approach of this how-to book is in workbook format. The introduction section describes and illustrates four kinds of resumes with chronological, analytical, functional, and imaginative approaches. The next section of the workbook illustrates what resume might be most appropriate for a specific job-hunting situation, such as mature woman, graduating college senior, military retiree, high school graduate, etc.

Women

Bird, Caroline. *Everything a Woman Needs to Know to Get Paid What She's Worth*. New York: Bantam Books, 1973.

This book, written in question and answer format, is a good handbook for any woman wanting to know how to deal with any job inequity. The answers are specific. For example, procedures are outlined for dealing with equal pay and equal opportunity cases. Information and advice is also given for such varied issues as how to get a bank loan, how to get into apprentice programs, and special tactics to use to get a promotion. An excellent annotated resource section is the last chapter in the book.

Friedman, Sande, and Lois Schwartz. *No Experience Necessary: A Guide to Employment for the Female Liberal Arts Graduate*. New York: Dell Publishing Co., Inc., 1971.

An excellent guide for the female college graduate who is uncertain about what she can or wants to do in the working world. The biggest portion of the book consists of fourteen chapters describing career fields that are most accessible to females with liberal arts degrees. Fields include advertising, the art world, banking and finance, book publishing, government, magazine and newspaper publishing, nonprofit, personnel and training, public relations, television, radio, and travel. Each chapter includes a general description of the field and notes several illustrative positions. Information is also given on which beginning positions are most likely available; advancement possibilities; and salary ranges. Each chapter lists specific sources of further information. Job-hunting techniques and part-time employment possibilities are both given some attention.

Jobfinding Techniques for Mature Women. Washington, D.C.: Women's Bureau, U.S. Department of Labor, 1970.

This brief guide gives step-by-step assistance to the mature women in preparing for and finding employment.

Scobey, Joan, and McGrath, Lee Parr. *Creative Careers for Women: A Handbook of Sources and Ideas for Part-time Jobs*. New York: Essandess Special Editions, 1968.

Describes how to combine professional interests with domestic life in a flexible career. Includes information on starting one's own business and finding a job. Suggests sources of additional information.

Seed, Suzanne. *Saturday's Child*. New York: Bantam Books, 1973.

Interviews with women in 36 different jobs are compiled in *Saturday's Child*. The different jobs represented were chosen because they are predicted to be growth fields in the future as compared to some of the common female jobs (teaching, nursing, librarian) which are expected to be overcrowded in the future. The fields represented include: arts and communications; science and medicine; trades, services and businesses; and commerce and government. As one reviewer states, "This should provide a shot in the arm for girls interested in pursuing any of these rewarding careers."

Schwartz, Felice N.; Schifter, Margaret H.; and Gillotti, Susan S. *How to Go to Work When Your Husband Is Against It, Your Children Aren't Old Enough, and There's Nothing You Can Do Anyhow*. New York: Simon and Schuster, 1972.

This book includes lively profiles of women in varying martial situations who have found the right job for using their energies and abilities. Also, this is a good source of information for employers of women. A section in the second half of the book identifies positions and professional associations of interest to women.

International

* Angel, Juvenal L. *Dictionary of American Firms Operating in Foreign Countries*. New York: World Trade Academy Press, 1971.

Includes data on more than 3,000 American corporations operating overseas. Arranged alphabetically with cross references both by geography and product. If you want to work overseas for a business, this source is the place to start.

Calvert, Robert. *A Definitive Study of Your Future in International Service* New York: Richards Rosen Press, Inc., 1969.

Contains a discussion of careers with religious, voluntary, and governmental organizations overseas. There is also a chapter on teaching opportunities abroad.

Hopkins, Robert. *I've Had It*. New York: Holt, Rinehart, and Winston, 1972.

Subtitled "A Practical Guide to Moving Abroad," the book discusses the problems and advantages of moving abroad. The author relates the cycles that some people might experience if they actually make such a move. These include an initial period of elation, followed by a period of despondency and considering moving back to the U.S., and finally a period of leveling off when one realizes the disadvantages and advantages in their chosen environment. Information is included on job availability, taxes, climate, schools, and language training. Also included are lists of sources of books, pamphlets, and guides.

* *International Yellow Pages.* New York: Reuben H. Donnelley Corp.

Lists business and professional firms and individuals from 150 countries throughout the world under headings which are descriptive of the projects and services they have to offer in world-wide trade. English, French, German, and Spanish language versions. Divided into six geographical areas: Africa, Asia, Australia and Oceania, Europe, Latin America, Caribbean, North America. Lists businesses and organizations of an international character.

Researching Aids

* *College Placement Annual.* Bethlehem, Penn.: College Placement Council, Inc. Published annually.

This reference is available at college placement offices as well as many public libraries. One of the most useful tools for any college graduate seeking employment, the *Annual* contains information on United States employers that hire college graduates. Information given on each employer includes the following: brief description of the nature of the business or organization, name of the college recruiting officer, number of employees, and occupational openings for which the organization will recruit. The *Annual* is indexed by academic disciplines and geographical areas.

* *Encyclopedia of Associations. Vol. I: National Organizations of the U.S.* Detroit: Gale Research Co., 1970.

A comprehensive list of all types of national associations arranged by broad classification and with an alphabetical and key-word index. Gives name of chief officer, brief statement of activities, number of members, names of publications, etc. National associations can often give useful career-planning information as well as specific help in a job search.

* *Encyclopedia of Business Information Sources*. 2 vols. Detroit, Mich.: Gale Research Co., 1970.

This two-volume encyclopedia is a good beginning source to use to find out where to seek further information on a business topic. The first volume is arranged alphabetically and the topics range from the abrasives industry to zoological gardens. Under each topic, specific statistical sources, price sources, handbooks and manuals, periodicals, and trade associations are listed for further information. The contents in Volume II are for those interested in international business information, and the contents are arranged by geographical location from Africa to Zanzibar.

* *Federal Career Dictionary: A Guide for College Students*. Washington, D.C.: United States Civil Service Commission, 1973.

If you want to consider the federal government as an employer and you have an undergraduate college degree, start with this publication. It should be available in your local library or in any college placement office. The *Dictionary* is divided into three parts:

I. Description of federal career occupations

II. Description of federal agencies

III. Job briefs listed by college major

Read this before taking the Federal Service Entrance Examination. For those who have a graduate degree contact your regional Federal Job Information Center and ask for information about mid-level positions in your area of speciality. Those with a community college degree or high school diploma should contact the Information Center for publications relevant to your background and experience.

Greenfield, Phyllis O. *Educator's Placement Guide*. Washington, D.C.: National Center for Information on Careers in Education, 1972.

This small guide gives a wealth of information, including:

- Current trends in educational staffing needs
- Addresses for certification information by state
- Services of state education associations
- Services of professional and private agencies
- Addresses of independent, federal, international, and innovative schools

- Information on non-teaching careers (e.g., educational publishing houses, regional educational labs, research centers)
- Sample application letters and resumes

* *Industrial Research Laboratories of the United States.* National Research Council. Annual.

Contains information on 5,237 nongovernmental laboratories devoted to fundamental and applied research and operated by 3,115 organizations, mostly industrial firms. It includes fields of research interest and names of research and development executives. There are both subject and geographical indexes. Those with a science or technical background will particularly find this helpful for names of potential employers.

* Lewis, M., ed. *The Foundation Directory.* New York: Columbia University Press, 1971.

Directory of nongovernmental, nonprofit organizations established to maintain or aid social, educational, charitable, religious, or other activities serving the common welfare. The two criteria for inclusion in the directory are: (1) awarded grants of $25,000 or more in that year, (2) total assets of $500,000 or more. This directory is useful in investigating foundations as potential employers and also for preparation of proposals for grants to determine possible support. It is indexed alphabetically by state and by fields of interest.

* *Macmillan Job Guide to American Corporations.* New York: Macmillan, Inc., 1967.

The guide offers a broad look at major American corporations—their goals, personnel requirements, and opportunities. Four areas covered in the guide include:

- Description of corporations and job opportunities. (This includes information on annual sales, employees, mission and products, facilities, degree requirements, opportunities, and benefits.)
- Alphabetical index to corporations
- Index to corporations by college degrees
- Geographical index to home offices

This book is a good place to find out what companies are seeking persons with a particular type of college background.

* Pingree, E., ed. *Business Periodicals Index*. New York: The H. W. Wilson Co., 1971.

Indexes approximately 250–300 journals covering a wide range of industries. Excellent general reference for researching a company or an industry. It is indexed alphabetically by company and by industry, and it lists all articles within a given year relating to a particular company or industry. The index is also useful in identifying trade journals for a given field.

* *Research Centers Directory*. 3rd ed. Detroit: Gale Research Co., 1968.

A directory of approximately 4,500 research institutes, centers, foundations, laboratories, bureaus, and other nonprofit research facilities in the U.S. and Canada. It is arranged by type of research done. Excellent for identifying research organizations in any field (social science, education, biological science, physical science, business and industrial relations, etc.) Information includes scope of research activities and names of publications, sources of funding, and the names and addresses of principal researchers. This directory would be helpful to those wanting to work in a particular research area or for identifying names of people who could be helpful in a job search.

* *Thomas Register of American Manufacturers*. 11 vols. New York: Thomas Publishing Co., 1971.

These eleven volumes contain detailed information on leading manufacturers throughout the country. Included in the set are:

Vols. 1–6—Products and services listed alphabetically

Vol. 7—Company names, addresses, and telephone numbers with capital ratings, names of company officials, and locations of branch offices

Vol. 8—Brand names

Vols. 9–11—Catalogs of companies appearing alphabetically and cross-indexed in first eight volumes.

* U.S. Bureau of Census, *County and City Data Book 1972*. Washington, D.C.: U.S. Government Printing Office.

This publication will enable those involved in job searching to gather statistical information on thirty items of interest when changing environments. Information is indexed by county, city, metropolitan area, urbanized area, unincorporated places, regions, divisions, and states.

* Wasserman, Paul, and Greer, W. R., Jr. *Consultants and Consulting Organizations*. New York: Graduate School of Business and Public Administration, Cornell University, 1966.

> This is a detailed listing of consulting firms arranged alphabetically and cross-referenced by subject field and geographical location. This could be helpful in a job search in locating companies doing independent consulting in your area of expertise. They could be considered potential employers or persons who could describe the feasibility of starting your own consulting firm.

* *West Coast Theatrical Dictionary*. Los Angeles: Tarcher/Gousha Guides, 1971.

> Contains information on companies related to the entertainment industry in Los Angeles, San Francisco, Nevada, and Hawaii. There are also alphabetical listings for Chicago, Nashville, and New York. The main sections of the directory include artists representatives, broadcasting/radio and television and associated services, live show production and distribution, motion picture and TV production equipment, facilities and services, music, recording, tape and associated services, public relations/advertising, graphics and associated services, publishing and associated services, theatrical instruction, unions, guilds, and trade associations. For those interested in the entertainment industry this is a good source.

PARENT-CHILD PROBLEMS

Dreikurs, Rudolf, with Vicki Soltz. *Children: The Challenge*. New York: Hawthorne Books, 1964.

> An easy to read self-help presentation of Adlerian-Dreikursian approach to resolving parent-child conflicts. The book is directed primarily toward developing skills in handling one's self when in conflict with children eleven years of age and younger. However, the principles apply to any age level of relationship. Examples clarify the various principles presented. The appendix includes a series of exercises for testing the extent to which the reader has mastered the skills described in the text.

Soltz, Vicki. *Study Groups Manual*. Chicago: Alfred Adler Institute, 1967.

> A manual designed to assist parent study group leaders in coordinating the information appearing in *Children: The Challenge* with study group deliberations. Especially suited to assisting lay leaders who have a

propensity for "leadership" but need assistance in organizing the particular content. Includes techniques for leadership, study topic outlines, and discussion-promotion questions.

Dotson, Fitzhugh. *How to Parent*. New York: New American Library, 1970.

A collection of suggestions and advice regarding how to be an effective parent for children from birth through age five. Dotson writes from the point of view that while parenting is one of the most complex occupations in our society, there is no formal training by which one can prepare for it. His book is an attempt to provide some of that training. Especially helpful are appendixes listing toys and play equipment, free and inexpensive toys, and parents' guide to children's books for preschool children.

Ginott, Haim. *Between Parent and Child*. New York: Avon Books, 1969.

Written in a light, easy-to-read style. *Between Parent and Child* illustrates the point of view that communication is the key to "settling the undeclared wars which so often leave both parents and child angry, confused, and regretful." The volume contains many specific examples of using open communication to solve specific problems. It could be particularly helpful for parents who truly can't see why their children behave as they do. The examples are realistic enough to provide a basis for parents trying some of Ginott's suggestions.

———. *Between Parent and Teenager*. New York: Macmillan, Inc., 1969.

Very similar to Ginott's *Between Parent and Child* except the focus is on problems likely to arise during adolescence, including rebellion, authority, conflict and crisis, identity and autonomy.

Gordon. Thomas. *Parent Effectiveness Training*. New York: Peter H. Widen, 1970.

Like many other books regarding parent-child conflict, this one places a great deal of emphasis on communication. It describes and illustrates several methods for resolving parent-child problems and conflicts. Basic to parent effectiveness training is the concept of democratic discipline, wherein family rules are established which are acceptable to parents and children alike. Gordon's examination of concepts such as authority and discipline should be revealing, thought provoking, and helpful to many parents.

RETIREMENT

Arthur, Julietta K. *Retire to Action: A Guide to Voluntary Service.* Nashville: Abingdon Press, 1969.

Today's retirees are of the work-oriented generation so the suggestions in this volume may mean more than all the guides on recreational opportunities. The author has done a very thorough job of exploring volunteer opportunities and the information resources available to the retiree.

For those who are accustomed to viewing volunteering as envelope stuffing, there may be some exciting vistas—even VISTA.

Collings, Kent J. *The Second Time Around: Finding a Civilian Career in Mid-Life.* Cranston, R.I.: Carroll Press, 1971.

As the title indicates, this book is on target for a special population —the retired military. Much of what Mr. Collings has learned since his own retirement, however, is useful to the increasing numbers of the middle aged who are looking for changes. Because Mr. Collings's style is spritely, his observations acute, and his honesty refreshing, this book is fun to read, retiree or not.

Cooley, Leland Frederick, and Cooley, Lee M. *The Retirement Trap.* Garden City, N.J.: Doubleday, 1965.

The Cooleys are out to instruct the unwary on the pitfalls in retirement. They are primarily concerned with housing choices. However, as in most retirement guides, the concern is life-style. "Through darkest retirement with gimlet and screwdriver," says the bartender in one retirement village when he characterizes the lost souls he "counsels." The need to be needed cannot be dismissed lightly. Retirement villages, they believe, are filled with the unneeded.

Hart, Mollie. *When Your Husband Retires.* New York: Appleton-Century Croft, 1960.

While most retirement preparation books are written for the employed person, this one, as the title indicates, aims at helping wives anticipate retirement irritations. The author writes, "From now on this is going to happen every day. Not just Saturday and Sunday but every Saturday and Sunday and every other day of the week too—forever. Wow!"

Hepner, Harry W. *Retirement—A Time to Live Anew*. New York: McGraw-Hill, Inc., 1969.

    This is one of the best books available on retirement planning. It is addressed primarily to the businessmen who have no great worries about retirement income. Written by a retired psychology professor, the book is a gold mine of information, guidance, and good sense. Mr. Hepner's ability to provoke sound thinking should be of great value to all persons approaching retirement so that they can plan on a realistic and effective basis for the later years. It can be equally helpful and stimulating to those already retired.

McKain, Walter C. *Retirement Marriage*. Storrs, Conn.: Storrs Agricultural Experiment Station. University of Connecticut. 1969.

    Marriage at sixty plus is not a subject about which much is written. This report of research is presented in lay language. Indicators for success of late-life marriage are listed and the book includes a self-administered test for predicting successful retirement marriage.